BE YOUR OWN HOME CONTRACTOR

BE YOUR OWN HOME CONTRACTOR
How to build your dream home and save money too

Edward M. Walsh, B.Comm., LL.B.

Self-Counsel Press
(a division of)
International Self-Counsel Press Ltd.
Canada U.S.A.

Printed in Canada

First edition: December, 1995

Canadian Cataloguing in Publication Data
Walsh, Edward M. (Edward Michael), 1941-
    Be your own home contractor

    (Self-counsel how-to series)
    ISBN 0-88908-847-0

    1. House construction — Specifications — Popular works. 2. Construction contracts — Popular works. 3. Housing — Finance — Popular works. I. Title. II. Series.
TH4815.W34 1995   690'.837   C95-911003-8

Cover photography by Terry Guscott, ATN Visuals, Vancouver, B.C.
Figures prepared by Don Doneff

Self-Counsel Press
(a division of)
International Self-Counsel Press Ltd.

Head and Editorial Office	*U.S. Address*
1481 Charlotte Road	1704 N. State Street
North Vancouver, British Columbia V7J lHl	Bellingham, Washington 98225

To my mother and other extraordinary women like her who create homes out of houses.

CONTENTS

APPENDIXES

GLOSSARY

FIGURES

INTRODUCTION

Many Canadians dream of building or renovating a home. In order to fulfill such a dream, you don't need a lot of background in building construction. All you need to do is properly assume the role of building contractor and use the information in this book.

You can create from sticks and stones a valuable investment which you can someday leave behind just as generations before have done; many fine homes built in the early 18th century still stand today. Also consider the thousands of dollars you can save by keeping the builder's profit and overhead expenses down. True, most professional builders get discounts off the cost of materials that are sometimes not available to you, but that's a small portion in relation to the overall savings you get by contracting the project yourself.

Contractors hire tradespeople who actually do the building or renovating. As a general contractor, you can hire trained subcontractors (tradespeople) who are specialized in the various building jobs. Also, as general contractor you ensure that the best materials are used for attaining quality work.

By reading this book, you will discover how to hire the best people and how to benefit from their experience and know-how. Building is similar to other fields of endeavor such as health services. How many executive hospital directors are knowledgeable and experienced in surgery? Take another example such as automotive retailing and repair. How many owners of automotive franchise operations are thoroughly knowledgeable about parts and repairing automobiles?

You don't have to know every minute detail. Directing the co-ordination of services is surely the essence of successfully turning dreams into reality. Leave technicalities to those who have spent years gaining working knowledge and experience. The subcontractors have put in the time to learn their specialty by attending training schools, apprenticeship programs, and on-the-job experience.

This book explains step by step what you need to know to build or renovate a home. Chapter 1 lists the advantages and disadvantages of building yourself, as well as what you need to perform the role of owner-builder.

In chapter 2 you learn about the three types of building lots and their relative advantages and disadvantages. Also discussed are the benefits of land concepts and land rights; how to assess a neighborhood; how to conduct a site analysis; and how to submit a conditional offer to purchase while you finalize your investigation.

Chapter 3 shows you how to locate the building area inside the legal boundaries of the property.

In chapters 4 and 5 you learn how to assess house designs and floor layouts. There are five basic house designs, and guidelines are provided for examining the best house elevation and designs that suit different lot shapes and topography. You learn to assess the floor layouts that meet your needs and wants.

In chapter 6 you learn how drawings and plans are reproduced to a convenient scale. Blueprints and their symbols are explained for interpretation of those drawings.

House plans are only part of the building documents. You need more documents when you file for a building permit. Chapter 7 discusses the importance of building documents.

Chapter 8 is for the renovator planning an addition to an existing home. Vertical and horizontal additions are identified and you learn about how your house is affected by solar orientation after a renovation.

As a builder, you must know who the participants are in the building process and when they get involved in each phase of building. Chapter 9 provides this information.

Chapter 10 outlines how you can investigate subcontractors and material suppliers. Use the rules suggested for tendering jobs and learn how to locate and investigate tradespeople and select the best quotes.

After selecting the best quotes, you enter into contracts with the subcontractors. Chapter 11 provides three easy methods for getting your terms and conditions accepted as a written contract. Major problem areas are cited and solutions are listed.

Before determining whether you can secure enough financing for your project, you need to prepare a budget. Chapter 12 guides you step by step to help through the details of doing so.

All building projects are doomed without financing. You need to know where and how to get money to build. Chapter 13 guides you through the interim financing and the mortgage take-out process.

When you've completed the preliminaries and you want to start the actual construction you must apply first for a building permit. Chapter 14 gives you an idea of what you might expect. The bureaucracy you're up against depends on the type of building lot you own. You cannot always go directly to the chief building official and demand a building permit.

Chapters 15 to 19 cover the actual building steps in a sequential order. The building stages are broken into five convenient phases with an appendix accompanying each phase for assisting you to identify who you need to contact for co-ordinating each subcontractor and material supplier.

The final chapter contains information for setting up a maintenance program after you have settled into your new home. By implementing a program of checking, cleaning, and repairing, you can experience the comforts of home ownership and extend the life expectancy of the house's component parts.

There is a glossary at the end of this book. Refer to it for builder's terms that come up throughout the book.

I've paid my dues; I've confronted just about every surprise conceivable after building over 400 homes. Learn from my mistakes by following this guide. I wish you and yours the best of luck. Empower yourself with the knowledge and the suggestions contained in this book.

1

BEING YOUR OWN HOME CONTRACTOR

Home contractors are hired to turn dreams into reality. Traditionally, if you wanted to build your own home you contacted a builder who acted as the contractor. The contractor hired the subcontractors who supplied all the materials, equipment, and labor, which meant you had little contact with the subcontractor.

As an owner-builder, you get the opportunity to fulfill your own dream. That's exciting. But you need to evaluate the pros and cons, assess yourself, obtain knowledge, listen carefully, contract properly, and co-ordinate and supervise others. You also need to implement a work schedule to keep on top of the work.

First, review the following basic advantages and disadvantages to your venture.

a. TYPES OF BUILDER'S CONTRACTS

There is no such thing as a standard building contract. Here are descriptions of three common types of contracts builders are likely to use if you hire them instead of acting as contractor yourself.

1. Fixed price contract

A fixed price or predetermined lump sum contract sets out the price the owner pays for the scheduled work. This figure could be spread over payments or paid as a lump sum at a predetermined time(s). It means the owner is buying the house or addition at a predetermined price. The fee includes labor, materials, equipment, as well as an allowance for contingencies, overhead, and profit.

This type of contract is well suited for small- or medium-sized jobs where the work is relatively straightforward and the chance for any major surprise is slight.

2. Cost-plus contract

With a cost-plus contract, the owner pays for the actual cost of materials, labor, equipment, and a percentage or fixed fee to cover the builder's overhead and profit. This type of contract is used where the job cannot be accurately estimated because the owner can't or doesn't describe the full extent of the work required in advance.

The cost-plus contract is often problematic for the owner because there is little incentive for the builder to carry the work out economically, and the full cost of the house or addition will not be known until the job is complete.

3. Design-build contract

Design-build contracts are popular where a builder is chosen before the design or plans are prepared. The owner supplies three or four builders with a set of design requirements and the builders, in turn, submit a tender based on preliminary design.

Usually the owner isn't knowledgeable enough about design or construction so he or she will hire an architect or building manager to assist in the tender to bidders and the selection from various proposals.

This type of contract is suitable for large projects. Design-build contracts should be written on a fixed price. However, if the only alternative is a cost-plus basis, then it is wise to have a guaranteed upper limit.

As an owner-builder, you stay in control and you get to prepare contracts to deal directly with the subcontractors by eliminating the builder. That's exciting!

All you need to do is to empower yourself with knowledge, listen carefully, contract properly, co-ordinate and supervise others. Implement a work schedule, keep on top of the work, and you'll succeed.

b. ADVANTAGES OF BEING YOUR OWN HOME CONTRACTOR

There are a number of advantages to being your own home contractor. Obviously you've thought of some or you wouldn't be reading this book. Below are some advantages you might not have thought of yet.

1. You are the boss

There is pride and excitement in being the boss. You can drive up to your job site where machines are hustling and bustling. People are milling around, and you've caused it all to happen. Sub-trades are seeking you out for answers, the neighbors are curious, and the air is filled with excitement. Your dream is coming alive.

2. You arrange the timetable

You set the timetable and determine the pace. Whether you are in a rush or you want a slow, steady construction period, your schedule determines when other people work. You decide when you want a task completed and you can choose when is a good time to take a vacation when you're not needed.

3. You choose everything

You can pick the materials, determine the various standards of quality, and decide which subcontractors to work with. This gives you an opportunity to make special deals, save more money, negotiate better quality, and opt for alternative specials without paying extra charges to a builder.

4. You can make last-minute changes

Last-minute changes are unavoidable. When you work with builders, changes involve extra charges from the subcontractor to the builder and eventually to you the owner. Their charge usually has a 10% or 15% mark-up over the cost for the change, and the owner's request for the change automatically triggers a change in the contract between the builder and the subcontractor. But as an owner-builder you can save most of extra fee that builders charge.

Because you deal directly with subcontractors, they have to justify their extra charges, and they're less likely to back-charge for every conceivable change.

5. You get the recognition

You can have the satisfaction of saying, "I did it." There is a tremendous feeling of accomplishment after you tell your friends and relatives that you were the builder. You can say that you controlled the quality and design during every step of the process.

6. You can save thousands of dollars

Added to the joys of having fun turning your visions into reality, you have the opportunity to reap the tremendous financial reward for your efforts. By careful planning and by assuming the role of builder, you can earn the contractor's profit as well.

c. DISADVANTAGES OF BEING YOUR OWN HOME CONTRACTOR

As with everything in life, there is a down side. Worthwhile goals aren't achieved easily and that includes turning your dreams into reality.

1. You have full responsibility

You must accept full responsibility for everything that goes wrong. You can't hide or blame someone else; the buck stops with you, regardless of who is at fault. You will have to pick up your pride at times, and your pocketbook as well.

2. You have to plan and decide in advance

Often, building involves planning and making decisions in advance. Later you may wish you had the chance to do things differently. Sometimes that's discouraging but, as with everything worthwhile, you have to see it through no matter how painful it may seem at the time. In the end it is worthwhile.

3. Sometimes it isn't fun

Sometimes it's impossible to schedule sub-trades to start and finish exactly as you've planned. This can be frustrating, especially when subcontractors leave you hanging, inspectors take unreasonable positions, and material suppliers make mistakes. Surprises happen in the building industry; don't count on everything running smoothly all the time.

4. Sometimes subcontractors are scarce

Often subcontractors are difficult to find in specific geographical areas, particularly when building activity heats up. Good tradespeople are always working. It may be hard to hire them away from builders who keep them busy. You may have to place small ads in a local newspaper to recruit subcontractors.

5. Sometimes it can be stressful

Everyone will depend on you for decisions and answers. Also, unexpected problems, delays, and bad weather are the hallmark of this industry. You can't control everything, and when things go wrong, you cannot walk away.

Expect the unexpected. Subcontractors and material suppliers experience delays all the time. Delays cost money, but it's part of the building game. Just do your best, keep an open mind, and make the best out of tough situations.

d. ARE YOU A BUILDER?

There are some misconceptions about builders. In the past, builders carried a hammer and a saw. Now, builders are more like administrators and co-ordinators. They rarely get directly involved with the physical part of building. Builders should possess certain capabilities and knowledge.

1. Experience

Experience is helpful but not essential as long as you can manage tradespeople, listen carefully to others, and keep on top of the job until it's complete. While tradespeople are hired for their extensive technical knowledge about building, as builder, all you need to know is how to engage them and make sure they do a good job.

2. Administrative skills

Builders are like administrators. For instance, a hospital administrator utilizes properly skilled surgeons to perform operations, but he or she wouldn't tell a surgeon how to perform an operation. Similarly, a builder does not instruct an insulating subcontractor on how to commence work. Instead, builders need to know who to engage and when, which subcontractors are necessary, and in what order. You have to know the right time for starting each phase of work and then delegate that work properly.

3. Contract negotiating skills

Good business acumen starts with negotiating a good contract. This means ensuring you have written documents with business people you intend to deal with; everybody tends to forget what they said during negotiations. By getting a signed contract in black and white, you will have fewer problems, but the agreement must be clear and concise. Chapter 11 provides tips on getting the legal edge.

4. Conflict resolution skills

Disputes are inevitable when you are dealing with several subcontractors and material suppliers. Communication breakdowns or a misunderstanding of the scope of work causes many disputes. Building inspectors often reject methods of construction or materials in constructing. Sub-trades get upset after being told to make changes at their expense. The builder's contract might appear legally airtight, but does it mean subcontractors must bear the total loss for added time and costs to make material changes? In many circumstances, fault and responsibility is a gray area. You have to handle these disputes.

Builders, believing they have the strong hand, often refuse to solve disputes. Dissatisfied subcontractors may threaten lien action (a legal claim on the property of another in settlement of a debt) against the job site when forced to make costly changes and lose money without some form of compensation from the builder.

Learn to settle before lawyers get involved. Explain your position and negotiate. Be prepared to compromise. If you take a rigid stance, you will lose out on legal costs and interest charges. Instead, use those lost costs as part of a compromise. Subcontractors don't want to go to court, but they will.

So, by compromising and offering to pay to avoid a potential lawsuit, a cheaper course of action is chosen and delays are then minimized. Even if you are legally right, in the end, it's better to avoid legal costs and court proceedings.

5. Financial know-how

It is futile trying to turn dreams into reality without financial resources. You need personal assets, either in liquid form (cash or convertible securities) or in equity form as with an existing home that is eventually sold and turned to cash. What personal funds and mortgage financing is available for you to contribute to the project?

To determine how much mortgage financing is available, consult a financial institution and supply your personal financial information. A financial adviser will tell you the maximum amount of mortgage they're prepared to pre-approve on your behalf. (See chapter 13 for an excellent method of arranging interim financing to pay the building accounts while construction is underway, and for a method for maximizing mortgage financing amounts with as little as 10% of your own money invested.)

6. Estimating skills

You need to determine the maximum amount of money available for financing, then learn how to estimate to determine the size of house design that you can afford to build. Research what the basic square foot costs are for one- and two-storey homes in your area. Be aware that square foot costs are higher for one-storey than for two-storey designs; fixed overhead costs such as foundation and roofing are more costly than adding on another storey.

Mortgage officers, appraisers, builders, and renovators use estimated square foot building costs for valuing replacement costs or for estimating new home construction. By subtracting the land costs, the upgrades, and the sales commission from the builder's new home sale price, you can determine fairly accurately the building cost, which includes the builder's profit.

For one-storey designs, divide the total main floor living area by the net building cost to determine the estimated square foot cost. If the property includes a garage, don't forget to exclude its cost. By performing the same calculation for three or four homes, you can determine an average building square foot cost for one-storey homes in your area.

Let's look at an example. Suppose you see an advertisement for a builder selling a one-storey design for $163 000 which has a finished main floor area of 1 200 square feet. The builder has three upgrades:

(a) a fireplace valued at $2 500,

(b) a patio deck valued at $1 800, and

(c) an air conditioner valued at $2 000.

You assume that the builder pays real estate a commission of 4.5% of the selling price.

If you deduct from the selling price the total of the upgrades ($6 300), the commission (4.5% x $163 000 = $7 335), and the cost of the land ($50 000), you will determine that the net building cost including builder's profit (excluding garage cost) equals $99 365.

Now divide the living area (1 200 square feet) by the net building cost ($99 365). It equals $83 dollars (rounded) per square foot for a one-storey design.

To determine square foot costs for two-storey designs, perform similar calculations. Add the two living levels together and divide the total square foot area into the net building cost (exclude garage costs). Perform the same calculations for two-storey designs (use at least three comparables) to determine an average square foot cost in your area.

After you determined your building estimates, look into land estimates. Canvass the area to ascertain building lot prices. Land prices are meaningless if you haven't factored in all costs for services such as water, sewage, and hydro. (This aspect is discussed in more detail in the next chapter on purchasing a building lot.)

When you discover the cost for fully serviced lots, simply deduct this figure from your total assets available for building including pre-approved mortgage financing. For example, if you have $175 000 available to fund the building project representing cash and mortgage financing, deduct the land cost and the remainder is the reserve amount to contribute to the building cost:

Total funds available from all sources	$175 000
Minus the cost of land with all service costs added	$62 000
Reserve amount available for building costs	$113 000

If you decide to build a one-storey design and the average square foot cost is $83, then determine an affordable square footage area. Divide the reserve amount available for building costs by the square foot cost: $113 000 divided by $83 = 1 361 square feet.)

The cost for upgrades such as a garage, extra bathroom, patio deck, air conditioner, built-in appliances, fireplace, or cathedral design are not part of the basic square foot cost for building construction. To determine how many upgrades you can afford, take your reserve amount and deduct your building costs from it.

Of course, there is more available than just one- and two-storey designs. In chapter 4, we discuss how the square foot costs for one- and two-storey homes can be adjusted and implemented for the other designs as well.

7. Organizational and co-ordinating skills

Your ability to organize and co-ordinate the jobs in order to get ready for the next subcontractor gives you the edge. If subtrades know you are prepared, then word spreads quickly. They are less likely to waste your time. Keeping everyone informed of what is and should be happening is an essential job for the builder.

8. Listening skills and decision-making ability

Builders need to listen carefully and accept advice. Plans and specifications are prepared by professionals. Subcontractors transform drawings into a physical, functioning structure; they know from experience what works best and how to save time and money. Listen carefully and know when to accept their suggestions; often, deviations or variations from the plans can prove beneficial.

For example, heating and ventilation subcontractors might suggest that the heat ducts should be altered from the original plans. They may recommend straighter duct runs, which will provide more efficient airflow throughout the house.

After listening carefully and discussing suggestions with the sub-trades who are affected by proposed changes (such as the framer and plumber), the builder may then decide to deviate from the drawings. These situations come up, so as a builder you must listen to recommendations and decide whether to take action.

9. Improving your skills

If you are unsure about how strong your skills are for being your own home contractor, you can get help from the Canada Mortgage and Housing Corporation (CMHC) or the local library. Various articles and booklets are available, several of them published by the CMHC, to assist

→ Order lit from CHMC

home owners who decide to act as their own builder.

 In addition, CMHC has published a book, *Canadian Wood-Frame House Construction*, which has very helpful information concerning the technical aspects of house construction. This material can be ordered from a branch office of the CMHC.

e. CONSTRUCTION TIMETABLE

Do you have the time to take on this project? If you have decided to be a builder, then be prepared to devote a couple of hours during the evening and early morning to call subcontractors.

Co-ordinating a timetable is one of the key ingredients for completing the job properly and on time. As with all schedules, they're subject to revision; give yourself ample time between jobs.

During the construction timetable, keep your weekends open and arrange holidays around the latter phases of the construction project when most activity occurs.

Keep in mind what the weather forecasters are predicting. Also, keep communications open with your inspectors; they have their own idiosyncrasies which have to be pampered if not respected.

Now, let's proceed to turn your dreams into reality by examining the factors laid out in the next chapter.

2

BUYING A BUILDING LOT

After searching for building lots and speaking to realtors and perhaps developers, you are finally drawn to a particular parcel of land. You are interested, but you're not sure about making an offer just yet because something could go wrong.

Someone else might also be interested in the land; you're afraid they will buy it. People reassure you, but you still have mixed emotions. Do you jump in blindly? What if you can't get a building permit? What if there are hidden costs that blow out an affordable budget? Should you risk buying without investigating first?

To help answer some of these questions, read on and then follow the list at the end of this chapter before buying or entering into a commitment to buy.

Just because a building lot is advertised doesn't mean a building permit is automatically available. Some building lots advertised for sale require servicing, which involves unknown costs. With some land it's impossible to get a building permit. With others, you are involved with many preliminary approvals before the building department will look at your application for a building permit.

Land involves more than just space; land involves legal concepts. Land has rights attached, which are sometimes bargained off, taken away, or suspended. Governments, prior owners, present owners, and strangers can alter rights which in turn can affect the right to build.

Nearby areas are sometimes slated for future development, and if it materializes, it affects the neighborhood — sometimes negatively and sometimes positively. For example, when a major highway, factory, shopping mall, or apartment building is proposed for a large vacant field, the developers need municipal approval. You should investigate to find out whether such developments are allowed or whether they are even contemplated for the future. Don't wait until it's too late.

The ground contains different soil materials beneath the surface. A visual inspection says nothing about underground soils. How do you check buried material? Suppose the soil is wet, rocky, or contaminated. How stable is the ground at the bottom where footings and foundation walls are going to be placed?

When buying land, you need to make an offer in writing, and there are pitfalls to signing standard realtor forms. There is never enough time to complete all your investigations. Should you spend money investigating without tying up the land first? How do you prepare an offer in order to give yourself more time to investigate without committing yourself?

Get answers to these questions before buying land. Conduct a thorough investigation. Regardless of assurances, ask yourself if you are willing to bet your life savings on what sellers tell you. If you're not, don't buy until you complete your investigation.

a. THREE TYPES OF BUILDING LOTS

There are three types of building lots you are most likely to encounter during your search.

1. The rural lot

A rural lot is a parcel in the country. Although they are generally larger and less expensive than city or town lots, they usually have no municipal services.

You need to add servicing costs before you can make a price comparison. The cost of digging or drilling a well, the cost of bringing hydro into the property, and the cost of installing a sewage disposal system are services you need to price out. Those costs vary from lot to lot, so get preliminary estimates to see if they are in line with your budget.

2. The infill lot

An infill lot is land inside city or town boundaries, such as space available in between already-developed housing. This space sometimes accommodates one or more building lots. Municipal services are usually available, but check to see if the services are located at the property line or at the street level.

gas

To provide services to the lot line, you may have to dig up the street to connect water, sewer, and hydro lines. The added costs for this servicing and restoration work have to be factored as part of land costs.

3. The subdivision lot

A subdivision lot is part of a large parcel broken up into individual lots located inside city or town limits. The subdivision usually contains services to the property line for each individual lot.

Developers must apply for an approved plan of subdivision: a survey that splits up the larger parcel, showing each lot's individual measurements and the location of street patterns for access to each lot in the subdivision. When a plan is accepted and approved, the local authority sets conditions under a development agreement for providing services.

Above-ground services include the type and width of streets, curbs, gutters, sidewalks, street lighting, and landscaping. Underground services include water, sanitary sewer, storm sewer, gas, hydro, and other services trenched underground for the benefit of each individual lot.

After a plan of subdivision is approved and registered, the developer can sell lots. As part of the terms of sale, developers attach a building scheme (also known as building restrictions or restrictive covenants). Their conditions list a series of prohibitions or directions that builders or purchasers must conform to when buying. For example, there could be prohibitions concerning the size and design of the house, fencing, antennas, clotheslines, and specific uses on the property. (See Appendix 1 for a sample of the type of building scheme (restrictive covenants) intended to bind present and future owners.)

Developers sometimes set a time limit for commencing and completing the house construction. Builders or purchasers are required to post a damage deposit. The deposit funds are held as security against damages to curbs, sidewalks, water stands, and so forth. The deposit is returned without interest when everything is complete, no damage is evident, and the municipality assumes the subdivision.

b. LAND CONCEPTS

Land has legal characteristics distinguishing it from personal property. Understanding these legal concepts can help you in your negotiations.

1. The concept of uniqueness

No two parcels of land are identical, and since land is limited in quantity, those attributes give it a unique aspect. This helps purchasers in sale agreement situations where the developer wants to substitute the lot you intended to buy for a different one (he or she may have another buyer).

Courts endorse the concept of uniqueness by allowing purchasers to elect to force a vendor to perform the sale transaction as originally bargained. So if the purchasers are not satisfied with exchanging lots, it is possible to ask the court to force the vendor (developer) to complete the binding purchase and sale agreement for the lot they originally contracted to buy.

2. The concept of improvements

Improvements are objects affixed to land such as a house, barn, fence, or in-ground swimming pool. The physical condition of the improvement is irrelevant as long as it is attached to the land.

If you are buying land with a dilapidated barn or house, you should specify in your agreement who is responsible for the cost of removing the unwanted improvement; otherwise, the law assumes that the barn or house goes with the land. Nowadays, removal and demolition costs thousands of dollars.

3. The concept of natural resources

The concept of owning land includes everything attached on the surface of the earth, everything above it up to infinity, and everything below it to the center of the earth. This includes natural resources such as trees, streams, gold, oil, gas, and other minerals.

Land agreements therefore automatically include natural resources unless the wording of the purchase agreement states otherwise. That means vendors have no right to reap profit from the land's natural resources after a binding agreement is entered into.

By understanding land concepts, you may gain opportunities to negotiate to your advantage. You could sell the materials from a dilapidated barn or house to compensate for the cost of removal and demolition. Or, the land might have a valuable wood lot to sell off, thus reducing the overall land cost.

c. RIGHTS ATTACHED TO LAND

At one time, all land had specified rights attached to it. The rights included the right to sell, lease, build, mortgage, encumber, use, occupy, give away, share, will, mine, drill, and farm. Nowadays these rights could be suspended, limited, or abolished by acts of governments, owners, and strangers.

If the right to build is frustrated, then the land is worthless to you. So when you investigate building lots, determine if the right to build is in some way affected or abolished.

After conducting a search of title, your lawyer will point out where potential problems might arise when accepting title. There are certain areas to investigate to determine if the land you're considering is suitable for building purposes. This is in addition to the investigation your lawyer conducts. Let's begin by discussing how governments affect the right to build.

d. BUILDING PERMIT BEFORE CONSTRUCTING

Governments exercise control over building by granting or refusing to grant a building permit. So, your first concern is to determine if you can get a building permit. Then you need to know if there are conditions attached. You need a building permit before you can start constructing a home or a renovation project. Permission to build is not an absolute right.

Enquire at the municipal level to determine if a building permit is available; if not, ask what is involved before an application can be processed. Never assume that because land is advertised, permission to build was previously obtained. Investigate to determine if a preliminary clearance is needed before the building department will entertain your application for a permit to build.

e. PRELIMINARY CLEARANCES

In the following circumstances, preliminary clearances are often needed.

1. Land falls within a registered fill line or flood plain area

Government authorities control and police land located inside registered fill lines or designated flood plain areas. Fill lines are established to determine the location of setbacks for building and grading on slopes, ravines, and other areas. An application to build will not be granted in restricted areas. The same rule applies to land in flood plain areas. The purpose for the rules is to protect against land erosion, surface water run-off, floods, and natural hazards.

If building permits are available, they will be granted conditionally, when you can provide assurance that your proposed construction won't adversely impact the environment or be affected by natural hazards. You may need engineering or geotechnical reports to satisfy government regulations.

2. Land is without access to an established road or street

Be sure to investigate access; whenever the land fronts onto a major highway, access could be in question. Does the land have access to a street or road? If access is through a right of way, municipalities may require a right-of-way maintenance agreement.

3. Land is without municipal services

When municipal services are unavailable, the lot has to be serviced privately. For sewage disposal, the parcel must be large enough to accommodate a leaching bed. The government department of health or other environmental agency regulates private sewage systems. Before a permit to build is issued, a preliminary clearance concerning sewage is needed.

Normally an application with a diagram showing the layout and location of the sewage system is submitted to the appropriate government department or agency. A test hole of about five feet deep is dug and inspection is requested. The inspector assesses the quality of the soil to determine if the system will function effectively.

Also, an investigation is carried out concerning the size of the leaching bed, the system's location with regard to distances from other elements such as your proposed house, well, and the neighbors' houses, their wells, and nearby surface water. The authorities want to know what impact your sewage system will have on the surrounding area.

f. LAND RIGHTS BARGAINED AWAY

Sometimes prior or present owners bargain away rights attached to land. This may affect the right to build. Read on for some examples.

1. Granting a lease of land

When a lease of the property is granted for a term of years, it means possession is vested with a tenant. Therefore the land is unavailable for building purposes until the lease expires. If the land you are interested in is occupied for any reason, make sure your offer to purchase contains a clause that the lands are vacant on completion date.

2. Granting a right of way or easement

Past and present owners by virtue of ownership in land can grant a right of way or easement (see Glossary) to others for passage over part of their lands. This affects the right to build on areas reserved for right-of-way purposes. Only the remaining area uncovered by the easement is available for building purposes.

It is common to find a narrow strip of land over the back part of the property

reserved for a utility easement: access for hydro, cable, and telephone lines. Easements of this sort are necessary.

Sometimes utility easements cover not only the back portion of the land but the side portion as well. In this case, you might have to be content with a smaller building area. Check carefully into all utility easements because some can be troublesome for builders.

In addition to normal utility easements you may find another sort of municipal easement registered for an underground trunk line. This type of easement is not technically a utility easement but rather an easement for sanitary or storm lines which benefit the subdivision as a whole.

The design engineers may locate the main line over some of the lots in the subdivision instead of underneath the streets, which is the usual case. Presumably they chose the easement route because of gravity and costs for servicing under the street was determined to be too costly.

Unfortunately those lots become less attractive because the building area is further restricted and there is always the possibility that the easement area could be dug in the future if lines are plugged or damaged.

Easements are recorded in the office of public records against the title to the lands you're investigating. An up-to-date survey also shows the location of easements registered against the property.

3. Land with restrictive covenants

Sometimes land is sold with conditions that prohibit certain activities on the land. The prohibitions affect present and future buyers. (See Appendix 1 for an example of a restrictive covenant.)

Restrictive covenants are not confined to developers. However, developers attach prohibitions as part of a building scheme with the sale of subdivision lots to control building development and activities.

Be sure to investigate prohibitions and understand the impact they have on your lifestyle. You may be prevented from building a certain size or style home for example. You might not be allowed to park a recreational vehicle on the driveway. You might not be allowed to conduct business from your home.

g. GET A CONDITIONAL OFFER BEFORE ORDERING REPORTS

A conditional offer is like an option to buy. It enables you to tie property up for a period of time. You have an escape if you're not satisfied after conducting your investigations. Then, if a report comes back negative, you have the opportunity to either renegotiate or back out of the deal. All you've lost is time and the cost of the investigative reports. That's certainly cheaper than buying and discovering too late that it's going to cost thousands of dollars to solve a problem you could have avoided by not committing yourself on the dotted line.

If you need more time to complete your investigation, tell the vendors. They should accommodate you. In most cases you should get a reasonable period of time; if not, they may have something to hide.

Drafting a conditional offer is simple. All you have to do is state something like the following:

> This offer is conditional on the purchaser obtaining a satisfactory (soils or survey report, etc.) within ____ days of the date of

acceptance failing which this offer shall become null and void and the purchasers' deposit returned without interest. The purchaser may waive this condition by delivering a waiver notice personally in writing to the vendor within the time prescribed.

Make sure you put a condition in the agreement that the deal is subject to obtaining a satisfactory report. Protect yourself by eliminating doubts. Exercise caution and do not expose your investment to loss before the building ever gets off the ground.

h. REALTORS' STANDARD PURCHASE FORMS

Offers must be in writing. If you use a realtors' standard form of agreement of purchase and sale, read the fine print, especially where the agreement makes reference to easements and restrictive covenants.

The wording in many of those forms is troublesome. For example, most standard realtors' forms state that as purchaser you agree to accept utility easements and restrictive covenants running against the land. But part of your investigation is to research troublesome easements, especially utility easements, municipal trunk line easements, and prohibitions (restrictive covenants) you can't live with.

There is no sense in conducting an investigation if the fine print of the realtor's form obliges you to accept utility easements and restrictive covenants. Make sure that clause in the realtor's form is deleted or else you might be forced to agree to a developer's building scheme that prohibits all sorts of things you may not be able to live with.

i. INTERFERENCE WITH THE RIGHT TO OCCUPY

Sometimes third parties can interfere with your right to build. This may seem strange, but it occasionally happens. This is when the question of physical occupation becomes an issue.

Sometimes a lawful owner is dispossessed by a physical taking or occupancy by another. For example, if a neighbor constructs a fence or garage over adjoining lands, he or she is encroaching on land owned by others. If the real owner has not consented to the action, the neighbor's occupation is considered adverse possession.

How do you determine if a stranger encroaches on the land you're considering? Your lawyer can't help by searching the title because property records don't keep track of physical possession except for registered leases.

To discover encroachments, physically examine the location and determine where the boundary stakes are located, then run string lines from the surveyors' stakes.

If the survey stakes are missing, the only other way to discover an encroachment is to refer to an up-to-date survey, which may mean contacting a surveyor and having a new one done. Surveys reveal encroachments and easements and they show you their exact location.

Some jurisdictions adopt the old English law that says an owner loses to strangers, so-called "squatters," if an encroachment exists for a long period of time (in some jurisdictions ten years). After the time has expired, the lawful owner can be prevented from asserting his or her right to re-occupy those parts of the land where the stranger encroaches.

You can find out if your jurisdiction applies this law by checking with the office of public property records. The office of public records can tell you if the property is registered under the old English laws known as the registry system or the land titles system that generally prevents strangers from acquiring squatter's rights.

All encroachments restrict your building area. As a buyer, ask the vendor to remove any encroachment before closing the deal. Otherwise, expect a lot of hassle later from the neighbors when you try to get them off the property.

A current survey helps you discover encroachments and is a powerful document for establishing respective property rights and boundaries. This is important when encroachments are not so obvious by physically inspecting or when you can't use string lines from surveyor's stakes.

j. ASSESS THE NEIGHBORHOOD

Assess the neighborhood. Determine the permitted uses for the land you're considering and the surrounding properties. The municipality has specific laws concerning present and future uses.

Zoning laws prohibit certain land uses and set standards for setbacks, side yards, and rear yard clearances for building purposes. They control all sorts of uses. Zoning laws answer your questions about the uses you are permitted concerning the land you're investigating and the surrounding lands. For example, zoning tells you if you are allowed to carry on business in your home, what size of house can be built, or if neighbors are allowed to have a kennel.

Municipalities rely on an official plan, which is their stated objectives regarding future development for the area. It tells whether the vacant parcel of land across the street can be developed for a factory, a shopping mall, or whatever. Policies are generally stated through the official plan or through council policy statements. By examining official plan policies, you will have an idea of the type of development that is permitted on surrounding vacant land or adjoining properties.

Talk to neighbors and get their thoughts on the area. Ask about police protection; are neighbors experiencing break-ins and other crimes? What about noise problems or smelly air? If they are on well water, ask about the quality and quantity of the water.

k. CONDUCT A SITE ANALYSIS

What are the physical land characteristics? An examination of physical characteristics can have a bearing on the type, size, and design of home you want to build. Other physical analysis relate to soils. It's almost impossible to discover what's beneath the earth without a soils report.

1. Topography and grade

What is the contour of the land? If the land has steep grades, expect more costs for grading, filling, and retaining soil. You will also need more foundation material. Steep driveways can be a problem, especially during the winter season.

2. Availability of water

With unserviced lots a dug or drilled well is necessary. Enquire from local well drillers about the average depth where water was found, and the quantity and adequacy of well water. The department of health may have well water records for the area.

3. Soils condition

Soils relate to the type and adequacy of the material beneath the earth; soils cannot be examined by standing on the site, you have to dig. The condition of soil is important for determining its bearing qualities. The only way to know for sure is to obtain a soils report.

A qualified geologist digs test holes and examines the soil at different depths in the area where the excavation is proposed for footings and foundation. A soils report details the type of conditions and the adequacy of soils.

If the soil was previously disturbed and fill was placed on the site, then you have to pay additional costs for the excavator to dig further beneath the surface to find adequate bearing soil. The further you dig, the more it costs for materials, labor, and machine time to prepare the site for footings and foundation.

A soils report also gives an indication of how deep you must dig to find bearing soil, and the type of soil that's acceptable for placing footings and the foundation. It tells you the conditions your excavator will encounter during the excavation. For instance, if the soil is rocky, then expensive dynamiting might be necessary. If the land is within a high water table, then you may have a leaky basement.

If soil is contaminated or contains dangerous gases, a soils report is worth its weight in gold. It gives you an opportunity to re-negotiate the price or back out of the deal to avoid a nightmare.

1. RUN THROUGH YOUR CHECKLIST

Now that you have read this chapter, you should go through this checklist before committing to the building lot.

(a) What are the effects of different types of building lots offered for sale?

(b) Are there hidden servicing costs?

(c) Can the three legal land concepts prejudice or assist your position?

(d) What rights are attached to the land?

(e) Are provincial clearances needed before applying for a building permit?

(f) Have any of the crucial land rights been bargained away?

(g) Have any strangers interfered with the land rights?

(h) How is the neighborhood assessed?

(i) How is a site analysis conducted?

(j) When and how are conditional offers prepared?

Now you are ready to move on to the next chapter to explore how the building area is defined on your building lot.

3

LOCATING THE BUILDING AREA

By locating the building area, you can choose building designs, shapes, and floor layouts that fit. Some builders like to position the house close to the road to save costs for excavating and trenching service lines. Positioning the house toward the front also maximizes the amount of rear yard available.

But all these factors are practical considerations that take less priority than the legal limitations. Sometimes you don't have a choice after complying with the rules and laws.

a. LEGAL LIMITATIONS

What are the legal limitations that affect the location of the building area? At the municipal level, all land in some way is directly affected by regulations and by-laws. Municipalities will refuse to grant a building permit if you don't comply with them. In addition, there are regulations at other levels of government that only affect special circumstances. There are also other limitations of a property title nature that we discuss later.

1. Municipal by-laws

The municipal by-laws are a major concern for builders when defining the building area. Local councils set a whole series of rules for defining where to locate the house on the building lot. The applicable regulations are called zoning by-laws.

The building or planning department enforces these by-laws at the time an application is made for a building permit. Accompanying the plans and specifications is a plot plan showing the positioning of the house on the building lot. Zoning laws provide for minimum setbacks, maximum lot coverage, maximum building height permitted on land, and building additions.

(a) Minimum setbacks

The setbacks provide minimum distances for positioning houses and other structures away from property lines; they indicate where building locations are kept back by defining minimum front yard, side yards, and rear yard clearances.

For example, the zoning by-law affecting a particular property might provide for: the minimum setback for front yard 20 feet; the minimum setback for side yards 10 and 6 feet; and the minimum setback for rear yard 30 feet. Following the minimum setbacks, you could plot a preliminary building clearance area or perimeter inside the property boundaries according to the zoning law. See Figure #1 for an illustration.

(b) Maximum building coverage

In addition to the minimum setbacks, there is another rule pertaining to maximum lot coverage, which refers to the maximum percentage of ground floor area the house can occupy over the land. Suppose your building lot has a frontage of 70 feet and a depth of 100 feet. The area of land is 7 000 square feet. If the by-law states a maximum coverage of 30%, it means a maximum ground floor area for the house cannot exceed 30% or 2 100 square feet (30% of 70 x 100 = 2 100 sq. ft.).

Look again at Figure #1. The area shown represents the building clearance area of 2 700 square feet and somewhere inside that area you can build a maximum building perimeter of 2 100 square feet. Therefore a maximum of 2 100 square feet of ground floor area is allowed to be placed inside of the building clearance area.

After factoring in the maximum coverage, only 2 100 square feet of land coverage is allowed to be constructed on the land inside the clearance area. Figure #2 illustrates this point. The outside perimeter of the house shape cannot exceed 2 100 square feet. There is flexibility for positioning the house shape inside the building clearance area. Stacking one floor over another enables you to increase the square foot living area, which would be the case if you built a two-storey instead of a one-storey house.

(c) Maximum building height

Generally, zoning by-laws provide for maximum building height. The regulation rarely causes much problem unless the house is a two-storey with a high pitch roof. Different formulas are adopted for setting the maximum height. Some by-laws provide that the building height cannot exceed the total rear yard clearance. (Rear yard clearance is the distance from the back of the house to the rear property line.) For example, if the rear yard is 37 feet

from the house to the back of the property, then the height of the building cannot exceed 37 feet.

If the height restriction is based on the distance of the rear yard, then there is some maneuverability to increase height by moving the house forward to increase the rear yard distance as long as the minimum front yard clearance is maintained.

(d) Building additions

The zoning by-laws regarding clearances, maximum coverage, and height apply to additions to existing homes as well as to new construction. Plot any addition along with the existing house to determine if the remaining side and rear yard clearances comply. The new clearances created by the addition must comply with the existing zoning by-law.

For maximum coverage, add the square foot ground floor area of the existing home to the square foot ground floor area of the addition. The two areas together cannot exceed the maximum percent coverage for total building coverage permitted under the law. (See Figure #3.)

See chapter 14 for a procedure that is sometimes used to get around minor infractions of the zoning law. The procedure allows you to make a formal request for a variation. If the request is minor in nature then relief is generally granted.

2. Provincial regulations

Provincial regulations apply to special circumstances. Each province reserves the right to control various aspects of new house construction. These regulations pertain to special location lots, private sewage disposal systems, and other special circumstances. For example, land located on or near ravines, escarpments, wet lands, flood plains, and shore lines are generally affected by provincial regulations. Provincial regulations must be satisfied before the municipality gets involved with issuing a building permit.

(a) Ravine or escarpment lands

Where land is located on or near ravines or escarpments, you will find provincial environmental agencies establishing regulations affecting building activity. Fill lines are registered determining the limits beyond which building is prohibited. Regulations provide minimum setbacks and other measures for protecting the environment and safe guarding against the increased impact of natural hazards due to building activity in certain areas.

For example, in the case of a building lot partly located on a ravine, the regulations provide for a minimum setback from either a fill line or top of slope. This means the location of the building area has to be kept back from this line before building construction can be approved.

(b) Flood plain or wet lands

When land is located in or near wet lands or flood plain areas then provincial agencies responsible for regulating those areas may prohibit building altogether. In other circumstances building may be permitted within minimum setbacks from established contour lines. Building construction is discouraged where protective measures are futile against natural hazards, due to erosion and floods.

(c) Provincial highways and waterways

Land fronting on a provincial highway or waterway is generally regulated by a minimum setback usually more stringent than the municipal counterpart. An application is made to the provincial agency for special permission to construct. The agency responsible determines the minimum building setback. Before municipalities have authority to issue a building permit, the provincial agency has to grant special permission.

(d) Private sewage disposal systems

Building lots without municipal sewage require private sewage systems. Provincial regulations control the installation of the septic tank and field bed. These regulations potentially affect the building area because they require installations that are designed to have minimal impact on surrounding properties and surface water in the immediate area.

Municipal authorities cannot process a building permit application until clearance is obtained from either the department of health or another provincial environmental agency responsible for private sewage disposal systems.

3. Federal regulations

There are a few federal regulations potentially affecting building location. Those come into effect in rare situations, especially if the land in question is near a federally owned operation.

(a) Airport operations

Land near an airport operation falling within a noise exposure forecast or contour lines which run across a parcel of land might be affected by federal regulations. The regulations may require setbacks in order to avoid obstructing aircraft operations.

(b) Navigational aids

Building lots located near waterways that potentially obstruct aids to navigation under The Canada Shipping Act may place restrictions on building activity.

b. LEGAL TITLE LIMITATIONS

In the previous chapter we touched on easements, leases, encroachments, and restrictive covenants. These limitations may affect legal title to the land.

1. Easements

An easement is a right or privilege that one party has in the property of another that entitles the holder to a limited use of the property. If the title to land is subject to an easement, then other persons have rights over part of the land. Houses cannot be constructed on easement areas. Therefore, when locating the building area, watch out for easements because they can reduce the building area.

2. Leases

A lease is an agreement between a tenant and a present or past owner of land. Land subject to a lease is legally in the possession of the tenant and until the term of lease expires, building activity is restricted.

3. Encroachments

Strangers exercising adverse possession over lands owned by others without their consent are classified as encroachments. If there is some question, get an up-to-date survey to determine if there are encroachments against the land. Legal encroachments can prevent building activity in the area adversely possessed by the stranger.

4. Restrictive covenants

Restrictive covenants are conditions attached to land. They bind present and future owners to a list of specific prohibitions. As discussed in chapter 2, they are commonly associated with developers' building schemes. They might prohibit anything from a minimum square foot house size to the house's positioning on the lot.

c. SITE LIMITATIONS

Once you have defined the legal perimeters inside your building lot, you can position the location of the building structure on the ground as long as the positioning complies with the regulations.

The site limitations apply to the grade and to soils conditions. It is always preferable to position the house on high, flat ground. With steep grades, it costs more for grading, filling, and retaining the earth.

If a soils report discloses unsatisfactory soil or a high water table, re-position (if possible) the house away from problem areas. For example, if large concentrations of rock exist in specific areas, then it's prudent to re-position the house location to avoid costly dynamiting. The same rule applies for unstable soil conditions for footings and foundation walls.

The surrounding area may also have an influence on house positioning. For example, if all surrounding homes are built back off the road, you may be influenced to position the house to conform with the surrounding houses.

FIGURE #1
PRELIMINARY BUILDING CLEARANCE AREA

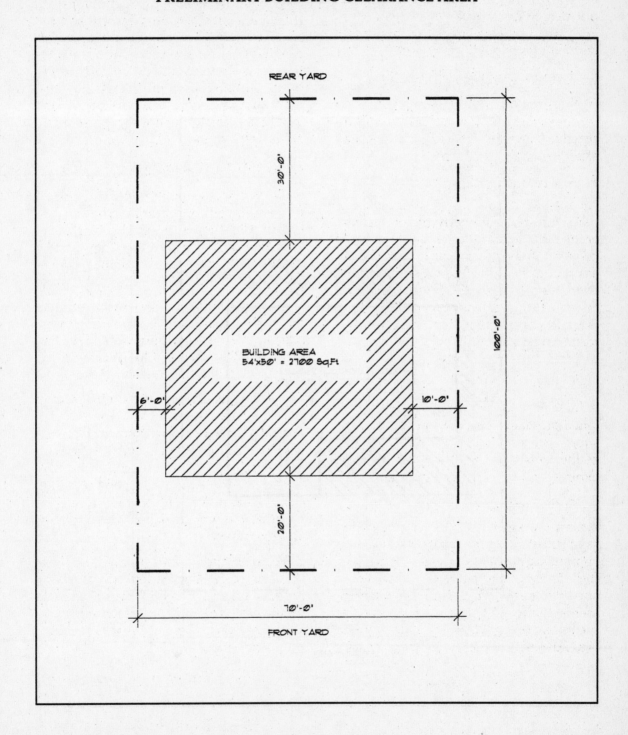

FIGURE #2
MAXIMUM GROUND FLOOR COVERAGE

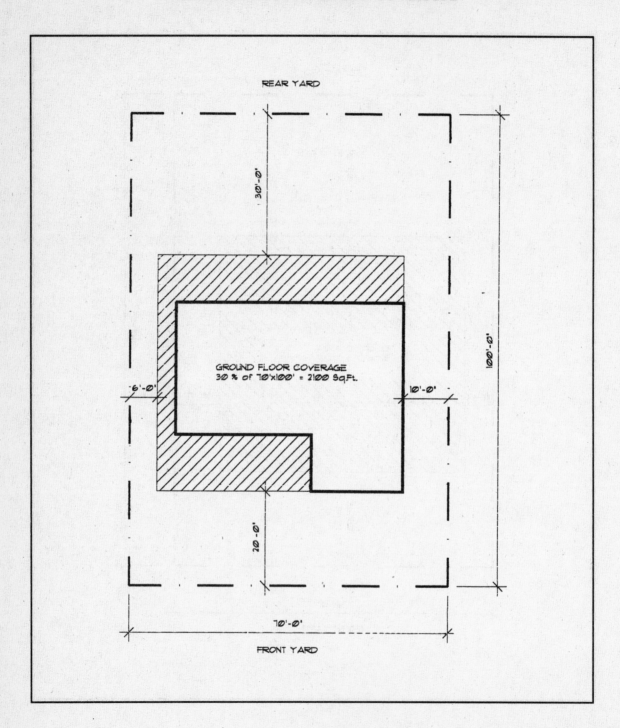

REAR YARD

30'-0"

100'-0"

GROUND FLOOR COVERAGE
30 % of 70'x100' = 2100 Sq.Ft.

6'-0"

10'-0"

20'-0"

70'-0"

FRONT YARD

FIGURE #3
MAXIMUM GROUND FLOOR COVERAGE EXISTING WITH ADDITION

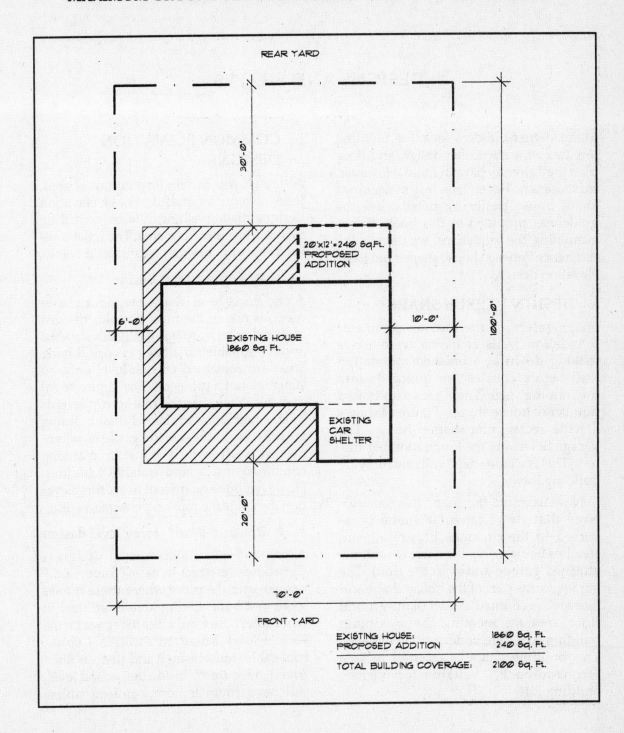

REAR YARD

30'-0"

20'x12'=240 Sq.Ft.
PROPOSED
ADDITION

100'-0"

6'-0"

EXISTING HOUSE
1860 Sq. Ft.

10'-0"

EXISTING
CAR
SHELTER

20'-0"

70'-0"

FRONT YARD

EXISTING HOUSE:	1860 Sq. Ft.
PROPOSED ADDITION	240 Sq. Ft.
TOTAL BUILDING COVERAGE:	2100 Sq. Ft.

4
DESIGNS AND SHAPES

Many owner-builders look for building lots to suit a particular design and floor plan they already have in mind. However, for those who haven't made firm decisions about house designing details, use the guidelines provided in this book. Before examining the guidelines, we discuss the difference between house shapes and basic elevation designs.

a. DESIGN VERSUS SHAPE

Shape refers to the outside perimeter foundation walls as if you were above looking down at a finished foundation wall before construction proceeds into the framing stage. There are an unlimited number of house shapes. Figure #4 shows a wide rectangular-shaped house. The garage fits inside the foundation perimeters. This is a side shape suitable for wide building lots.

Now examine the shape in Figure #5. Note that its rectangular shape is reversed to the previous illustration. Instead of being wide, it's narrow with the attached garage added to the front. The garage forms part of the house shape and that area is counted as part of the ground floor area for meeting the maximum building coverage under zoning by-laws. This building shape is referred to as a "front-to-back," suitable for narrow building lots.

b. COMMON ELEVATION DESIGNS

Although you can find numerous shapes, there are only a handful of basic elevation designs distinguishing houses according to living levels of floor area. The most common elevation designs are outlined below.

1. One-storey level design

A one-storey level (with or without a basement) is one of the most popular designs built today because it is easily constructed and it's suitable for all age groups. Living areas are contained on one level only, so stairs are not a problem. (See Figure #6 (a) and (b)). Note that the one-storey level is more suitable for a relatively flat building area. Access to the outside grade is accomplished easily, which helps for planning combined inside and outside activities. However, on a square foot basis, this elevation design is the most expensive to build.

2. One-and-a-half storey level design

A one-and-a-half storey level design is sometimes referred to as a "Cape Cod," named after the place where these homes were first built. Living area is utilized in what otherwise would be attic space on the second level. To attain additional space, roof gables must be high and steep as illustrated in Figure #7. Inside the second level, full head room is compromised unless dormers are added at the front or rear. Without dormers or skylights, natural lighting is limited to gable ends.

The design suits a flat building area and additional living space on the second level is accomplished without occupying more ground coverage. The additional living space is economical to finish on a cost per square foot basis because the structure is already in place.

The cost for the additional space could be less than one half of the basic square foot cost for building a one-storey level. To estimate a building cost, use one half of the basic square foot cost for a one-storey level and multiply it by the finished living area on the second level. For the first level use the square foot cost for a one-storey house and multiply it by the total living area on the first floor. Add the two calculations together for estimating a building cost figure.

3. Two-storey level design

Two-storey level designs have two living levels, one stacked on top of the other. Access is by a full flight of stairs leading directly from one level to the other as illustrated in Figure #8.

On a square foot basis, two-storey levels are less expensive to build than a one storey because the fixed overhead and the foundation costs of both designs remain the same, so the cost of adding a storey is less. We discussed a method for estimating preliminary building costs on a square foot basis in chapter 1.

Two-storey homes are suitable for flat building areas that are either small or large. With a small building area, you can build almost twice the living area on the same ground area as compared to a one storey. Generally, two-storey designs look stately if the boxy effect is eliminated by adding architectural styling and detailing to the exterior. It's well suited for large families that need several bedrooms on one level.

4. Split-level design

Split-level designs are a combination of the two-storey and one-storey levels connected by a series of less than full length stairs leading to three or four levels. Multi-levels provide a distinct separation of different living functions. This type of design opens up an unlimited variety of planned living spaces with the option of leaving areas unfinished until some future date.

A split-level suits both flat and sloped land areas as illustrated in Figure #9. Note the average height of the floor levels as compared to a two-storey where a full flight of stairs is required. Split-level designs are easily shaped as side level splits for wide lots or as front-to-back splits for narrow lots. On one level, the area contains a raised basement usually left unfinished for some future date.

To estimate a cost for three living levels, use this calculation: for the two upper levels, take the combined area (square feet) and multiply it by the estimated square foot building cost for a one-storey. For the lower (third) level use one half of the basic square foot cost for a one-storey level and multiply by the finished area. The two calculations when added together should provide an approximate building cost total for the split-level if all three levels are finished. Therefore, the cost for a three-storey house is two-and-a-half times the cost for a one-storey house.

5. Bi-level design

A bi-level design is a one-storey which utilizes part or all of the basement area as living space or as car shelter. This is achieved by raising the basement floor partially out of the ground, or by taking advantage of a sloped building lot where part of the basement is opened on the same level as the outside grade without extensive excavating. It enables you to utilize your land's topography and favorable soil conditions. Look at the bi-level designs in Figure #10; see how they utilize the basement area.

Whenever basement floors are raised as in Figure #10 (a), the raised ranch, footings beneath the ground must be located below the established frost level to prevent heaving the foundation walls in the winter. The condition of the soils at about four or five feet below grade must have adequate bearing soil for placing footings and foundation walls to maximize cost economy.

By raising footings and foundation walls, more foundation wall is exposed allowing for larger windows. With the basement raised, additional living space is made available at an affordable cost (approximately one half the cost of a one-storey level based on a dollar per square foot basis). Similar to Cape Cod Style

Figure #10 (b) and (c) shows designs that take advantage of a sloping lot. In the case of (b), the bi-level walk out, the lower level is converted to a walkout with easy access to the rear yard. If the building area slopes toward the street, the basement area is easily converted to a car shelter as illustrated in Figure #10 (c). The cost for a garage is substantially lower using this method as compared to building an attached or detached garage.

c. GUIDELINES FOR EXAMINING HOUSE ELEVATION DESIGNS

1. The shape and size of your building area

In the last chapter we discussed ways for determining your building area inside the legal boundaries of the building lot. Using information from zoning clearances and legal limitations, plot the building area.

Look again at Figure #1 in the last chapter. It's an example of how you prepare a plan according to a convenient scale and shows the building area inside the legal boundaries of your building lot.

2. The maximum building coverage allowed

Compute the maximum building coverage by first calculating the total area of your building lot. Enquire from the municipality what maximum coverage is allowed under the by-law. Remember the example in Figure #2. If the square foot area of the building lot is 7 000 square feet (frontage 70 feet x depth 100 feet = 7 000 sq. ft.) and the by-law calls for a maximum coverage of 30%, it means ground floor coverage cannot exceed 2 100 square feet (30% of 7 000 sq. ft. = 2 100 sq. ft.) which includes the garage area as well.

Maximum building coverage directly affects one-storey levels because the living area plus the garage area represents land coverage. But with other designs having more than one living level stacked over another, less ground coverage is needed.

3. The garage

Whether the garage is attached or detached, it counts for calculating maximum building coverage under zoning by-laws.

An attached garage as opposed to a detached garage might be more suitable for one design as opposed to another. Each case depends on the particular land characteristics, the size of the building area, the building area's shape, and the size of the garage. Remember, bi-levels and side splits might enable you to utilize the basement area for garage space or more living space to get around the maximum building coverage under zoning laws.

4. Your affordable building size

Chapter 1 discussed a simple method for determining a building budget figure using liquid assets and available mortgage financing. A method for estimating building costs for one- and two-storey homes in your area was also outlined. Now you have a method for calculating all five basic house designs.

Let's summarize how you determine a preliminary estimate for the one-and-a-half storey, side-split, and bi-level designs.

Measure the outside perimeter foundation shape excluding the garage. Calculate the area in square feet and don't forget to add for any cantilevers (see Glossary). Use the average square foot cost for a one-storey level and multiply it by the floor area.

For additional living levels, calculate the finished area (using outside measurements), which includes wall thickness. Take one-half of the basic square foot cost for a one-storey level and multiply it by the additional area you want to finish. Add the costs together for an estimated total building cost.

Now add land costs for estimating the total project cost and determine if it is within your affordable range.

The calculation of estimated square foot costs does not include a garage. If you plan for a garage, contact builders or renovators in the area. Obtain an estimated basic square foot cost and multiply it by the garage size you plan to build. Add the estimated garage cost to the total project cost.

5. Topography and soil conditions

If the building area is relatively flat, then examine which elevation designs are preferable. Building areas with severe slopes suit split levels and bi-levels. They are generally cost effective and you can take advantage of the land's topography. Review the illustrations provided in this chapter, keeping in mind the location and severity of your building area's slope and soil conditions.

6. Recreational activities

Are you combining inside and outside recreational activities? Some designs, like one-storey levels, are more adaptable for this purpose. With sloped grades, other designs might be more suitable for combining access to the existing grade.

7. Privacy from neighbors

Privacy usually plays an important role when selecting a design. To maximize privacy, select elevation designs that provide a shield or buffer against neighbors.

8. Designs that blend with the area

House designing should reasonably conform and blend with the existing homes and landscape. Imagine how each of the five basic designs fit on your lot. Take advantage of sloping lots whenever possible. Select designs that suit the land's topography. Also keep in mind the estimated building costs, especially when working with a tight budget. Later your efforts will be rewarded with a pleasing, attractive, and economical design.

FIGURE #4
RECTANGULAR HOUSE SHAPE ON A 70' x 100' LOT

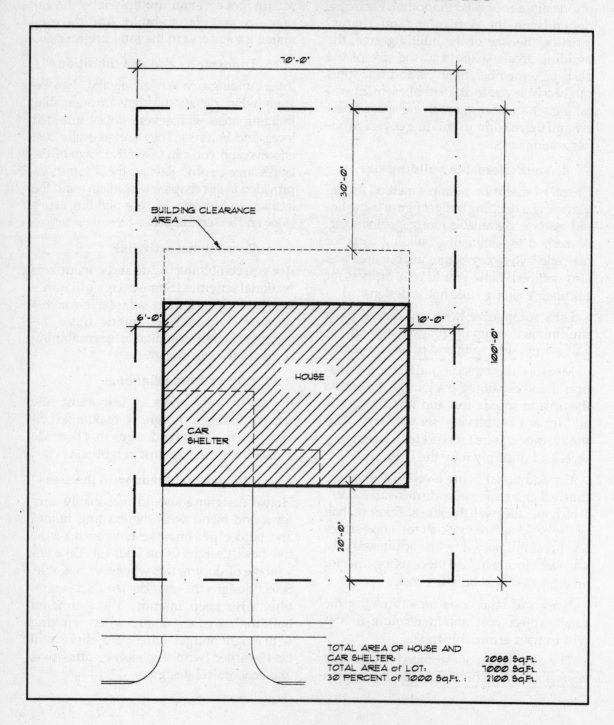

FIGURE #5
RECTANGULAR HOUSE SHAPE ON A 70′ x 100′ LOT
(Front-to-back shape)

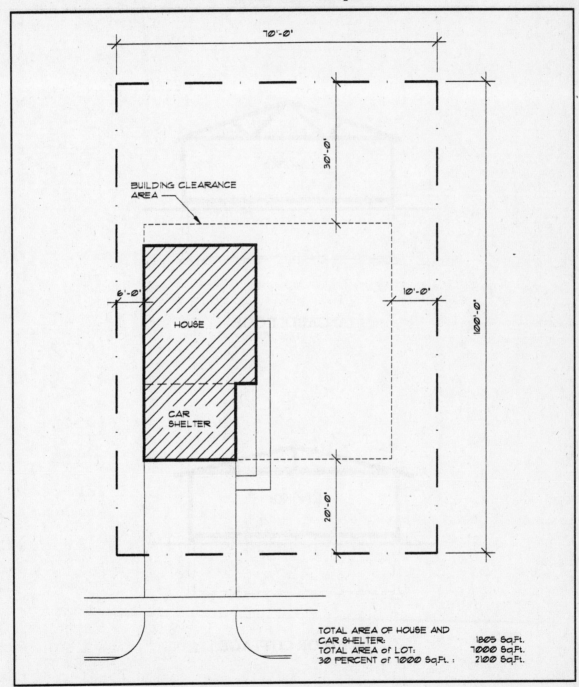

BUILDING CLEARANCE AREA

HOUSE

CAR SHELTER

70'-0"

30'-0"

6'-0"

10'-0"

100'-0"

20'-0"

TOTAL AREA OF HOUSE AND
CAR SHELTER: 1805 Sq.Ft.
TOTAL AREA of LOT: 7000 Sq.Ft.
30 PERCENT of 7000 Sq.Ft. : 2100 Sq.Ft.

FIGURE #6
ONE-STOREY DESIGNS

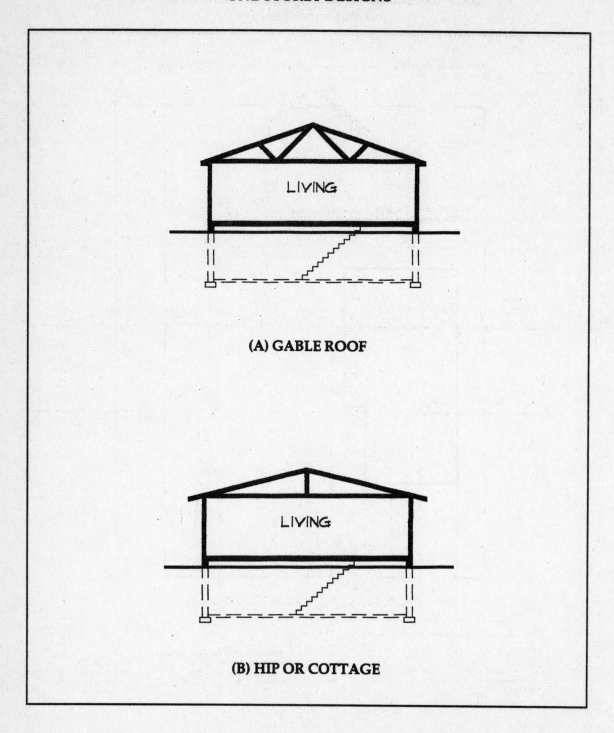

LIVING

(A) GABLE ROOF

LIVING

(B) HIP OR COTTAGE

FIGURE #7
ONE-AND-A-HALF STOREY DESIGN

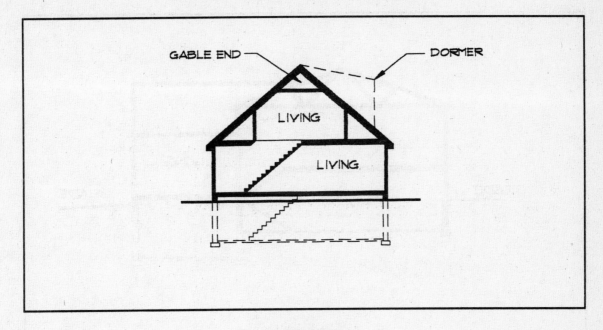

FIGURE #8
TWO-STOREY DESIGN

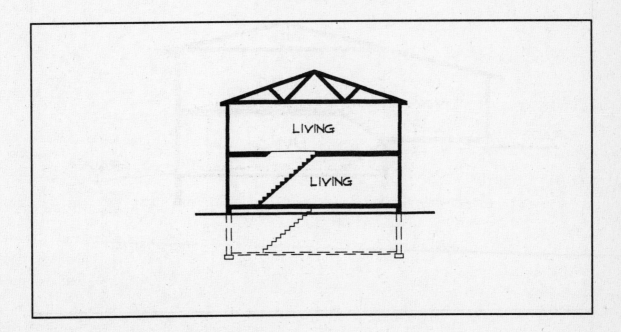

33

FIGURE #9
SPLIT LEVEL DESIGNS

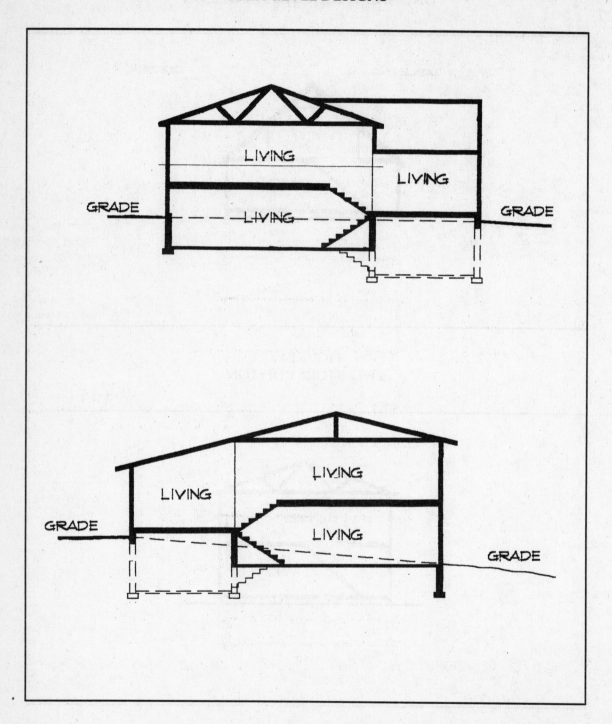

FIGURE #10
BI-LEVEL DESIGNS

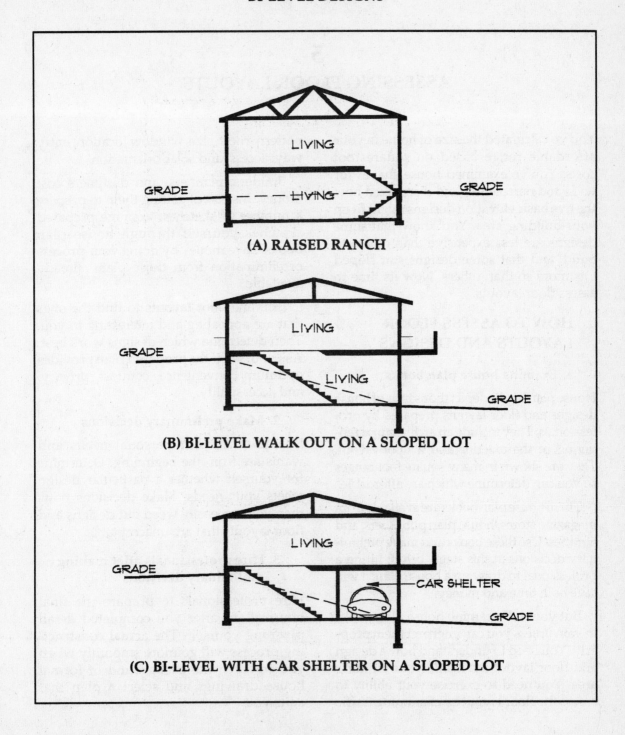

(A) RAISED RANCH

(B) BI-LEVEL WALK OUT ON A SLOPED LOT

(C) BI-LEVEL WITH CAR SHELTER ON A SLOPED LOT

5
ASSESSING FLOOR LAYOUTS

You've calculated the size of home in your affordable range based on square foot costs. You've examined house shapes for wide and narrow lots and discovered how the five basic elevation designs might fit on your building area. You know that some designs are less expensive than others to build, and that some designs suit sloped lots more so than others. Now its time to assess floor layouts.

a. HOW TO ASSESS FLOOR LAYOUTS AND DESIGNS

1. Examine house plan books

House plan books depict thousands of house designs and floor layouts prepared by professionals. They include an architectural rendering of the exterior and a floor layout. They are shown in many square foot ranges so you can determine which are affordable.

These house plan books are available from magazine stores, house plan publishers, and libraries. Use these books and make preliminary decisions at this stage, before hiring a professional to draw up a house plan; it will save both time and money.

But you will examine house plan books in vain unless you can interpret them properly. You need to understand how a design and floor layout fits inside your building area. You need to exercise your ability to assess the floor layout by examining traffic pattern, room size, window location, entry way, access, and solar orientation.

Builders, planners, and designers cost money. Instead of getting them to prepare a number of sketches, examine prepared sketches yourself through house plan books. Save money by doing your process of elimination from those plans already available.

Examine floor layouts to find the ones that are appealing and interesting to you. Then determine which designs work best. Ask yourself if the proposed plan provides optimum convenience, comfort, privacy, and accessibility.

2. Make preliminary decisions

Decide what your personal needs and wants are from the beginning. Determine for yourself whether a particular design meets your needs. Make decisions now, then you can easily weed out designs and floor layouts that are unacceptable.

3. Hire professionals after making preliminary decisions

Hire professionals to prepare the final house plans after you completed detail planning yourself. The actual constructing process will go more smoothly when you research the background of formal house drawings and select a plan that suits you.

b. CONSIDER YOUR LIFESTYLE

You need to identify your personal desires and lifestyle when determining your living space. To make the assessment of a floor layout easier, you need to consider the following factors and how they relate to the way you live.

1. The foyer or entry

The foyer is the first impression you get when entering the house. This area leads to the major living areas. First impressions last. Does the foyer appear spacious (not necessarily large) with adequate natural light? Does it have direct access to all major living areas of the home? Is the area shielded from other rooms such as the living room? Is closet space in close proximity for outerwear?

2. Traffic pattern

The foyer sets the traffic pattern. From this room you gain access to other living spaces in the house. Observe hallways or other forms of traffic pattern proposed for getting from one place to another. Does the traffic pattern make sense to you? Is there a hallway or some other means where you go through rooms to your destination?

Center hall plans are effective and work well, but other traffic patterns also work. Avoid layouts requiring you to travel through several rooms to get from one area to another several times a day.

Are hallways bright and wide enough? Does natural light have an opportunity to penetrate this space? Observe where the windows are positioned.

3. Living room

Does the living room serve for formal functions or is it intended for daily use? Does a larger space have to be provided for a lot of furniture and occupants? Do you want this room conveniently located at the front, side, or rear of the house? What about natural lighting needs during particular times of the day?

4. Dining room

What size dining room suits your furniture and the usual number of persons occupying it? Is the intended use for everyday meals, or just for formal occasions? Does this room have direct access to the kitchen? What about a temporary expansion that encroaches into other rooms for special occasions? Adjoining rooms where floors are stepped present a problem for expansion. Can you combine both dining and living areas to give an open and spacious effect?

5. Kitchen

Does the traffic plan in general provide easy access to the kitchen from the garage for unloading groceries? What about food preparation and serving — can this function be easily accomplished? Does the kitchen location provide a central network to the dining, breakfast, and family areas, as well as to the outside patio? Do you prefer having the kitchen open to the family room? Are the kitchen windows catching the morning sun? Is sufficient natural light available during the rest of the day?

6. Family room

Do you plan on having a family room? Have you considered combining family and living rooms together? How large does the family room need to be? Do you prefer direct access to the outdoors from this area?

What about a fireplace, should it be visible from other areas? What traffic pattern is planned from this room? Does this room need to be separate or open to other areas? How much wall or furniture space is available after allowing for a fireplace or television? What about natural light; where are the windows positioned?

7. Laundry area

Do you require a main floor laundry area? Is it conveniently located for easy access to the garage or outside? Could laundry facilities be combined with other uses? What about laundry tubs and shelving and cabinets — are they necessary? What about locating laundry facilities in the basement?

8. Bedrooms

How many bedrooms do you need? Will this requirement change in the near future? Bedrooms smaller than 9 x 9 feet are difficult to plan. What about locating the master bedroom away from other bedrooms? Does each bedroom have adequate closet space? Do you contemplate having an en suite bathroom off the master bedroom? Would a "cheater bathroom" (accessed directly from bathroom to master bedroom and hallway) suffice as a bathroom facility instead of an en suite? What about potential noises in close proximity of the bedrooms? How do the sun's rays affect each bedroom?

9. Bathrooms

Do you require more than one bathroom? Have the designers positioned the bathroom in a convenient and private location? Do you prefer a separate toilet compartment inside the bathroom itself? Where are the bathroom windows positioned? What about a linen closet? Do you prefer a separate shower stall and tub? Does the area provide easy access for the elderly or young?

10. Powder room

As a backup facility, this room is normally a two-piece bathroom conveniently located on the main floor. It is commonly found in two-storey level homes. Does this room have convenient access for both guests and family members? What about privacy?

11. Den/office

Where do you prefer to place this room? Does it have adequate closet space easily adaptable for storage? Can the area be converted to other uses?

12. Garage

Do you need a single, double, or triple garage? What about natural light in the garage area? Do you prefer doors leading to both the house and yard area?

For a single-car garage you need at least a minimum area of 9 x 20 feet and for a two-car garage, a minimum area of 18' 4" x 20' is needed. Does the garage have to be attached or detached? If attached, is the location preferably located on the side, front, or rear of the house?

Does the location act as a buffer for prevailing winds, the sun's rays, or privacy? Does the garage area have convenient storage available for riding mowers, landscaping, and gardening equipment?

c. COMPLETE A PERSONAL CHECKLIST

Using your answers to the preceding questions, devise a personal checklist to guide you in your selection of a design and floor layout that suits you. These are preliminary decisions you need to think about when planning living spaces. It's a flexible list; you'll probably need to make compromises on some areas. But the elimination process is easier when you've made these preliminary decisions.

d. PICTURE THE FLOOR LAYOUT'S SOLAR ORIENTATION

1. Examine the sun's path

Determine how the sun's rays strike various living areas during different times of the day. Where would the house design be positioned on your lot? Determine during different times of the day both in the summer and winter how living areas are affected. Take advantage of the sun's rays as they pass over the home.

Figure #11 shows the path the sun travels during the summer and winter seasons. From this information, visualize how the sun's rays affect different living spaces. Can comfort be maximized and passive solar heat gained through window size and positioning?

2. South facing windows

Living areas with south facing windows are warmer and easier to heat because of the direct accessibility to the sun's rays during winter months.

During the summer the heating effect from the south is reduced because the sun is higher and roof overhangs provide more shade from intense direct rays.

3. North facing windows

Rooms with windows facing north receive little direct sunlight. The light from the north is excellent for working and sleeping conditions. Natural light is dispersed evenly throughout most of the day. However, those rooms tend to be cooler.

4. West facing windows

Living areas with windows facing west may overheat during the latter part of the day. Windows from this direction provide bright living areas all year. Shade of some sort or smaller windows are required to avoid uncomfortable overheating and exessive light from the direct rays of the sun.

5. East facing windows

Living areas with windows facing east receive the benefit of early morning sun. Morning sunlight is often preferred for the kitchen and dinette area. Rooms used predominantly during the afternoon benefit as well from this position because they are not subjected to excessive overheating or light.

Observe the way the sun's rays shine into living areas during different times of the day. Whenever possible adjust window positioning and window sizes.

Research your needs and wants in conjunction with this preliminary procedure. Then examine floor layouts found in house plan books. You can select a plan that fits inside your building area, one that satisfies most of your preferences.

FIGURE #11
SUN'S PATH IN REFERENCE TO HOUSE POSITION

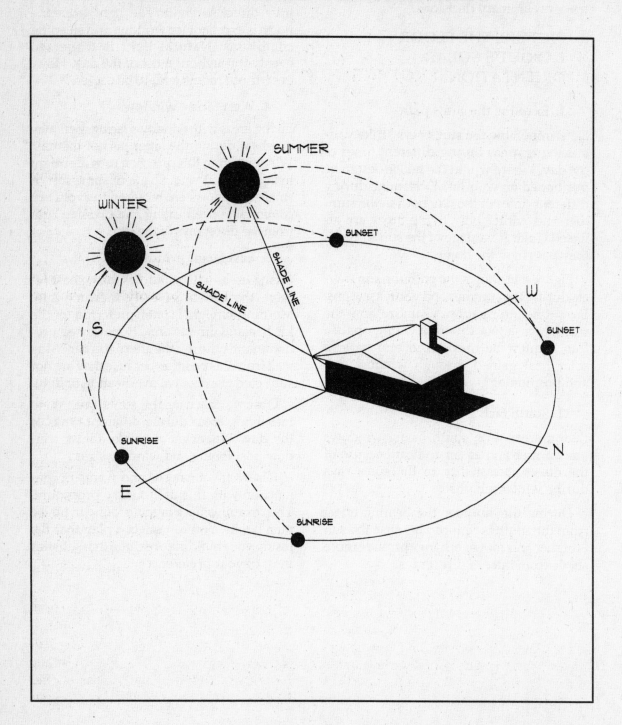

6
REPRODUCING PLANS TO SCALE

a. BUILDING LOCATION PLANS AND HOUSE PLANS

The two types of plans you need to familiarize yourself with are building location plans and house plans. Building location plans are sometimes called plot or site plans. They show on paper your actual building lot and house shape according to a scale. The location of the house is positioned in direct relationship with the building area and the building lot's boundaries. See Figure #12.

A building location plan is expressed on paper in a similar way as geographical areas are illustrated on a map. When you study maps you discover the way cities, towns, highways, waterways, mountains, and other areas are depicted; they are a series of lines and symbols drawn to scale with their location expressed in direct relationship to one another by distance and positioning to the magnetic north on a compass.

1. Scaling down your lot and house shape

Think of your building lot as a map. Think of it with the proposed house placed somewhere inside the building area which has a frontage and depth. Inside the building area the project is placed having distances measured from each boundary line and in direct relationship to the compass north as on a map.

2. Reference the street line to the compass position

The compass position of your lot is easily determined by the direction it faces toward the street. Streets are always referenced by compass direction running either north, south, west, or east. Picture the way the street runs across the front of your lot. If it runs in an east-west direction, then your lot faces either north or south depending on which side of the street.

3. Scaling building location plans

Draw the street line first to where your lot faces, and you can begin to mark off the front boundaries. The scale of one-eighth inch = 1 foot is convenient for drawing the location plans.

If you have a survey showing the dimensions of your lot, then it's simple to plot your lot on paper as illustrated in Figure #12 by following the surveyor's example. Take all of the actual dimensions for your building lot and reproduce them on paper reduced proportionately in size using the scale to fit.

If, for example, the frontage of a lot is 40 feet, then using a scale one eighth of an inch equals one foot, a line five inches long represents 40 feet and a line 12½ inches long represents 100 feet. This exercise should help you understand how to lay out your building lot and building clearance area according to scale.

When the lot boundaries are drawn, locate the building area. Examine Figure #2, which depicts a building clearance area, and review the information in chapter 3. Lay out the width and depth of the building area and then calculate the maximum building coverage for the ground floor area of the house shape that is allowed to fit inside this area.

4. Scaling house plans

House drawings show elevations, the foundation layout, floor layouts, and cross sections in detail, clear and large enough to read. Therefore, the scale is normally larger than for location plans and is normally one-quarter inch equals one foot ($\frac{1}{4}$" = 1').

If the actual size of a bedroom is 12 feet by 12 feet, then it is depicted on the drawing as lines 3 inches by 3 inches. Again, take the outside measurements for a house's shape (the foundation walls), and assume those measurements are 28 feet wide by 40 feet deep. On paper, the walls will have a line 7 inches long for the width and 10 inches long for the depth.

5. Reading scaled drawings

To understand scaled drawings, picture in your mind an actual size with its comparable scaled drawing size. The scaled size is an exact miniature reproduction.

Practice and familiarize yourself with a number of scaled rooms and furniture sizes; then compare them with their actual sizes. Examine the commonly used symbols used in drawings by drafters and architects (see Figures #17 and #18 in the next chapter). Familiarize yourself with their meanings. Eventually you will feel comfortable working with scaled drawings.

6. Blueprints

House drawings are referred to as blueprints. A print is an exact copy of the drawing. Originally, blueprints had a blue background with white lines, and were first printed in that fashion so they didn't fade when exposed to sunlight.

b. METHODS OF MEASUREMENT

There are two systems of measurement: the (English) imperial system and the metric system. The United States predominantly uses imperial measurement of feet, inches, gallons, and cubic yards. Canada, on the other hand, has been struggling to convert over to the metric system. Currently, we are in a mess because you will find both systems used: imperial measurement and metric measurement.

Because we're influenced so much by Americans, and because many Canadians still resist using metric measures, you may have to work back and forth between the two systems. Be sure to be consistent with your measurements; otherwise, you could end up with too much or too few materials or the placement of items could be off.

When you are dealing with government departments and municipalities, you will find the metric measures predominantly used. But for ordering materials and reading drawings and plans, both systems are used.

It is easy to convert from one to the other (see Appendix 16). In building construction, millimetre measurements are rounded off to the nearest full measurement. For example 1" equals 25 millimetres.

Some rules are numbered in centimetres, with ten small divisions (millimetres) between each one. However most rules show millimetres only. This is easier to read and leaves less chance for error.

In practice, architects prepare house drawings in millimetres. Site plans on the other hand are sized in metres. So for converting the metres into feet, generally you divide by 0.3048.

Building materials come in standard sizes, and most homes are built according to certain dimensional design standards. When the building industry converts to metric, new standards replace the customary ones.

FIGURE #12
BUILDING LOCATION PLAN OR PLOT PLAN

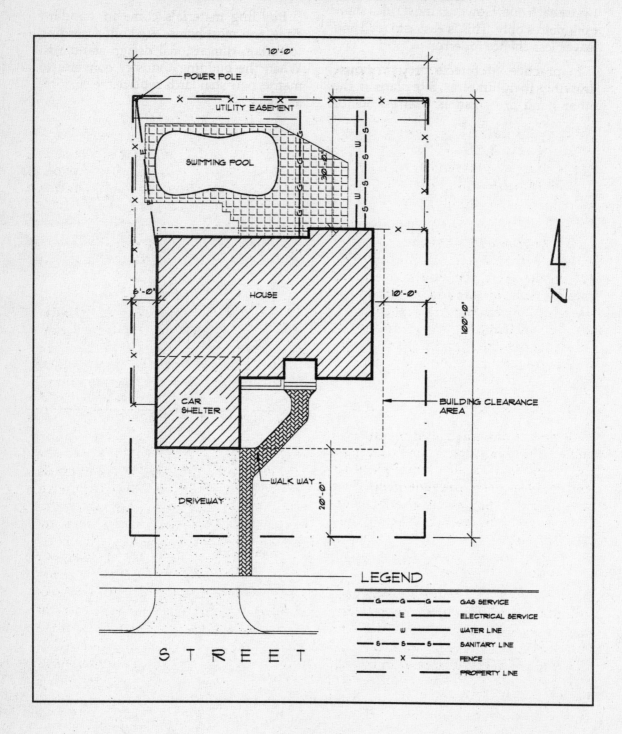

7

THE BUILDING DOCUMENTS

Building documents are more than just house plans. They are the documents you need in support of your application for a building permit. Without all of the documents you can't get permission to build.

As owner-builder, it is your responsibility to gather together all the building documents. They include house plans with detailed layouts and specifications, a heating layout, heat loss calculations, an optional truss (beams or other supports connected to support a roof) layout, a building location plan, and a grading plan.

a. HOUSE PLANS

House plans are obtained from architectural drafters, architects, or house plan publishers. Individually, house plans are made up of exterior elevation plans, floor plans, a foundation layout, exterior elevation plans, a cross-section diagram, and specification notes.

1. Exterior elevation plans

Elevation plans show a two-dimensional view of the home from the front, rear, and sides of the house (see Figure #13). The doors, windows, exterior wall covering, roof, and chimney are shown from each side of the house.

2. Floor plan

The floor plan (see Figure #14) contains dimensions showing the location of rooms, hallways, stairways, and closets. Inside the individual living spaces, dimensions show the location of walls, windows, doors, openings, electrical details, plumbing, heating, and built-in appliances.

3. Foundation plan

The foundation plan shows the foundation shape on top of the footings. It contains all the dimensions for the foundation walls, window opening sizes, door openings, beam pocket openings, concrete pad sizes, cross section, and notes (See Figure #15).

4. Cross-section diagram

The cross-section diagram details the house from top to bottom as if you sawed it through the center of the structure to open and examine it. Sometimes individual sections are shown for particular detailing. The details illustrate framing particulars, information about floor heights, stairways, connecting members between roof sections, wall sections, and details about how bearing weight is distributed from the roof down through to the footings. This diagram shows how various components form the structural integrity of the house.

This plan (see Figure #16) contains information for sub-trades and building code authorities who inspect the house during the constructing stages. The building inspectors use it to determine if the building techniques and materials used on the site comply with your plan.

5. General specification notes

General specifications are sometimes notes on a separate document. Sometimes they are included in each of the individual plans. When the notes form a separate document, they itemize a list of recommended materials and designating requirements for subcontractors to comply with standards of practice, code requirements, and building material specifications such as insulation, heating, ventilation, plumbing, electrical, and glass performance standards for the house.

6. Symbols used to interpret plans

Symbols are used to denote doors, windows, electrical wiring, heating, plumbing, and electrical fixtures and other details. Examples of symbols are shown in Figures #17 and #18. Familiarize yourself with those symbols so you can understand house plans and other building documents.

b. OBTAINING HOUSE PLANS

There are several sources for obtaining house plans. Some builders use architectural drafters or architects, while others buy stock plans from house plan publishers.

1. Using an architectural drafter

Most architectural drafters have limited education in architectural designing except for those who graduate from an accredited architectural technology program acceptable for membership in the Association of Architectural Technologists. Carefully check their educational credentials and experience before hiring them.

Find out their educational background in plans preparation and the number of house plans they have actually prepared. Who are their clients? They must be knowledgeable about the local municipal requirements where the building lot is located, and they must have a working knowledge of building code requirements relating to residential construction.

Architectural drafters base plan preparation costs on either a square foot basis or a flat fee. Compared to architects, their fees are economical. For a basic, simple house plan, they're the least expensive.

For complicated, untested house plans, you could find yourself in all sorts of problems if the drafters are not thoroughly knowledgeable about complicated stress and span requirements for house construction techniques. They may require materials which in effect over-build, and that alone can drive up material costs.

In other circumstances, vital information might be left out in the drawings, placing additional burden on a good framer to figure out how a particular detail is built. In the worst case scenario, you may be forced to hire an architect or engineer to solve the problem.

Architectural drafters don't normally extend guarantees concerning the methods or techniques they design, so you're left with little recourse if something goes wrong. However, that's not to say that there aren't excellent architectural drafters with extensive experience in the field of preparing house plans. A good percentage of builders hire their services. The experienced ones are now using computers, which eliminate most span or stress problems that arise.

Competent drafters are busy, working almost exclusively for builders, architects, and engineering designers. They may take considerable time to prepare your house plans. Consult them well in advance.

2. Using an architect

Architects are supposed to be specifically skilled and trained for laying out drawing details that work in the field. They specialize in building codes and complicated designing.

They are familiar with snow loads, bearing loads, and beam specifications; they can immediately determine if joining together components will provide the needed structural integrity for a good building.

Architects can save builders money by proposing building specifications that meet minimum code standards and at the same time keep material costs down by eliminating the necessity for over-specifying. They carry insurance to cover their mistakes so you have some protection if something goes wrong. However, architects charge premium fees for their innovative ideas and education. These fees range as high as 5% to 7% of the estimated house cost.

If you're planning on hiring an architect, make sure you have a good understanding about what you want to build. Negotiate the fee for services up front. Ensure that the architect's specialty is residential rather than commercial or industrial designing.

3. Buy a pre-designed house plan

Another way to obtain a house plan is to order stock plans from a house plan publisher. House plan publishers are easy to locate. Many advertise with toll-free numbers in magazines. They provide basic house plans that you need to get started.

House plan books have hundreds of house plans covering different styles, designs, and square foot ranges. Those books give for each house plan the building size, floor layout with room sizes, and a perspective showing how the house should look when it is constructed.

One of the largest house plan publishers in Canada is Select Home Designs. Their magazines are advertised throughout the country. For more information, call toll-free 1-800-663-6739. They have architects and building designers on staff. The cost for a set of their plans is reasonable and delivery is prompt.

The house plans they advertise are proven. Their plans are available on a reproducible vellum which enables you to customize them to your personal preference; simply erase and make your changes.

c. OTHER BUILDING DOCUMENTS

1. Heating layout and heat loss calculations

With the house plans you need a heating and ventilating subcontractor to prepare a heat layout and heat loss calculations. It costs less money for those documents if you get the same subcontractor who is doing the heating and ventilating work, to prepare this document

Using your house plans, they run specification and design particulars through a computer model to arrive at heat loss calculations which determine optimum efficiency for heating and cooling units. Figure #19 shows a heating layout.

2. Optional truss plan

Rather than framing a roof by the traditional stick build method using rafters, collar ties, knee walls, and ceiling joists, roof trusses as an alternative are often specified. With roof trusses you have to supply a roof truss plan. This plan is prepared by a roof truss manufacturer, usually the one who supplies your roof trusses. Roof trusses are manufactured off-site and delivered as component pieces when they are needed by the framer for assembly. Roof trusses or roof rafters hold up the roof sheathing and shingles (see Figure #20).

The bottom of the truss supports the ceiling finish, upon which ceiling insulation rests. (Examine Figure #21 which illustrates truss components as opposed to a rafter system shown in Figure #22.) The optional roof truss plan is filed as part of the building documents if roof trusses are specified in the house plans.

3. Building location plan

The site or building location plan shows the exact placement of the house inside the building area. The shape of the house contains measurements showing distances from the building lot boundary lines; a driveway location is marked out identifying where vehicles gain access to the street.

Other structures are identified, such as a detached garage, patio, shed, or swimming pool. Figure #12 in the last chapter is a building location plan illustrating the type of things you might expect to see in one of those plans.

Surveyors can prepare a site or building location plan. They are familiar with municipal set backs, easements, and other property restrictions, and they have experience drafting this sort of plan.

4. Grading plan

A grading plan shows how excess surface water is drained in defined directions according to a comprehensive plan for the area (see Figure #23). In new subdivisions, area drainage plans instruct how surface water is supposed to be drained from each lot.

Elevations are established and must reasonably be followed in the grading of lots in the subdivision. The direction of arrows suggest sloping for directing surface water by gravity. Each lot complies to the scheme of grading that's registered. You submit your grading plan with the building documents, which confirms that the lot grading on your lot will be substantially in compliance with the registered grading scheme, or if there is no grading scheme, then according to good drainage practice.

A surveyor prepares this plan, showing the house and improvements as they are proposed to be situated and affected by grading for complying with the overall plan or good drainage practice.

After gathering the building documents together you're ready to determine who the subcontractors and material suppliers should be. But before contracting, we discuss in the next chapter additions for renovators who plan on adding to their existing home.

FIGURE #13
EXTERIOR ELEVATION PLANS

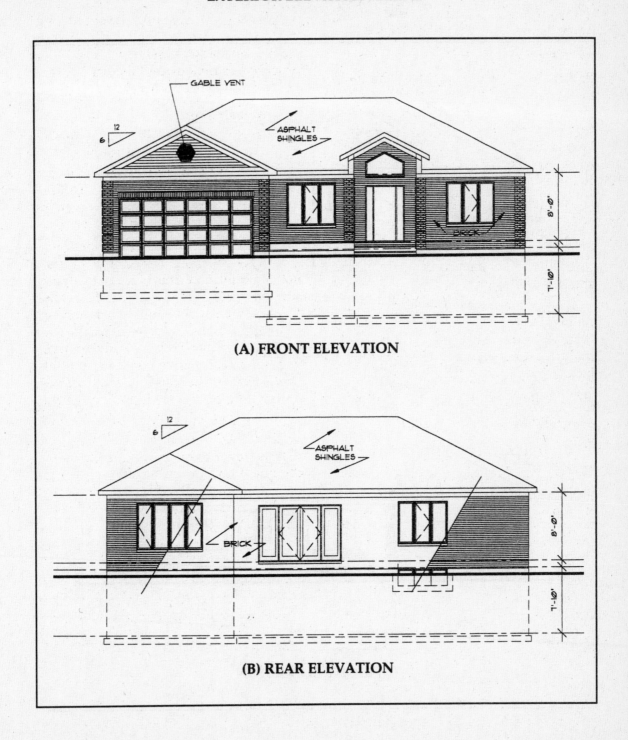

(A) FRONT ELEVATION

(B) REAR ELEVATION

FIGURE #13 — Continued

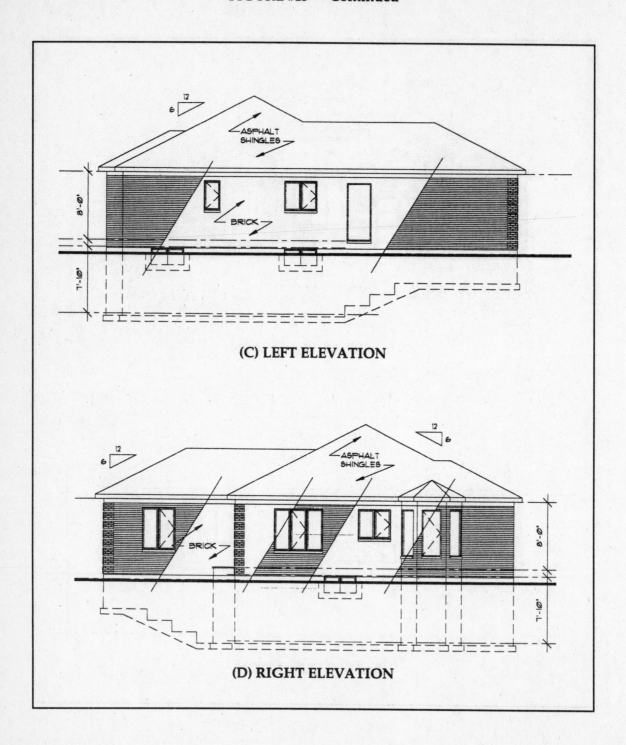

(C) LEFT ELEVATION

(D) RIGHT ELEVATION

FIGURE #14
FIRST FLOOR PLAN

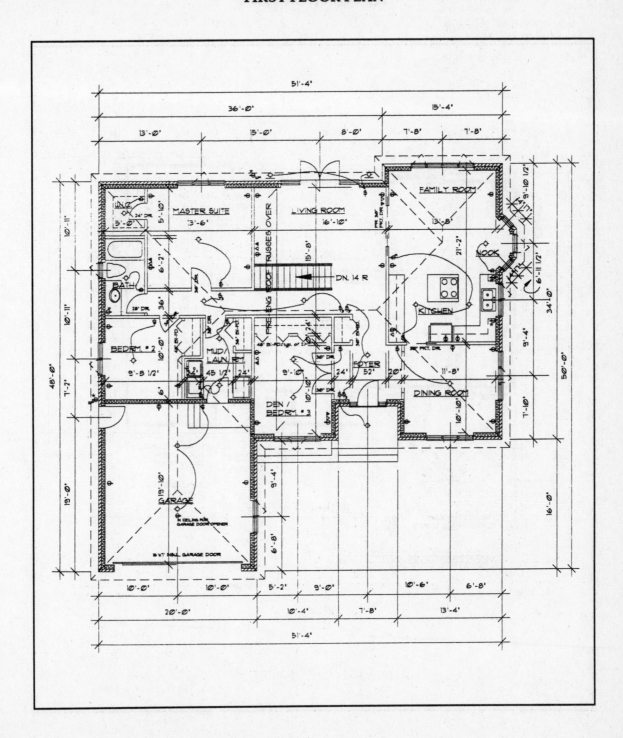

FIGURE #15
FOUNDATION PLAN

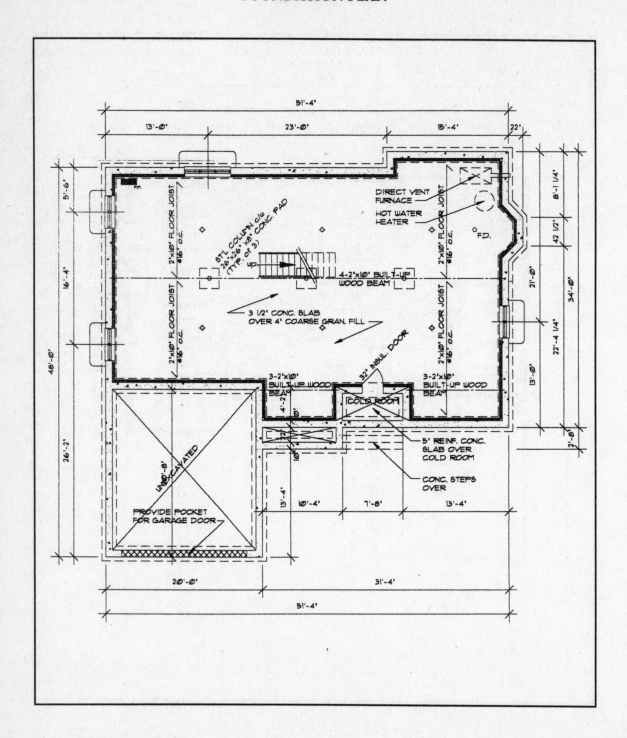

FIGURE #16
CROSS SECTION

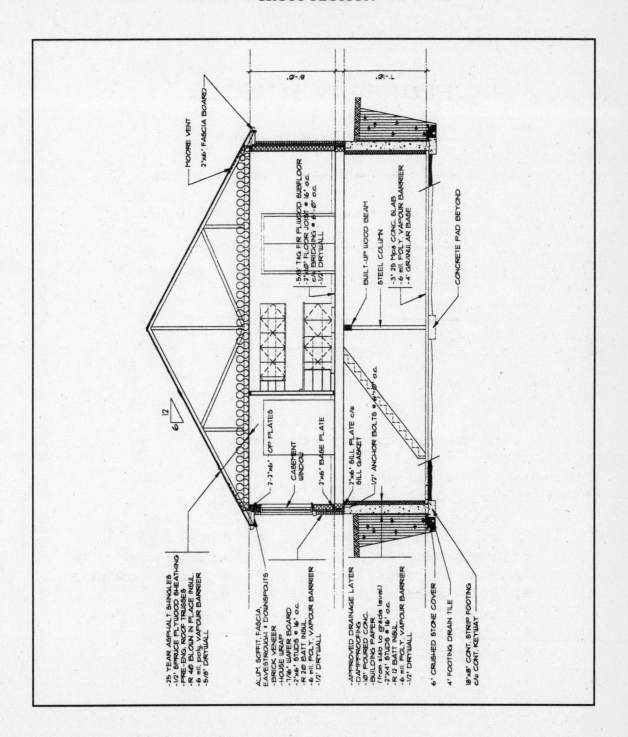

FIGURE #17
PLOT PLAN AND ELECTRICAL SYMBOLS

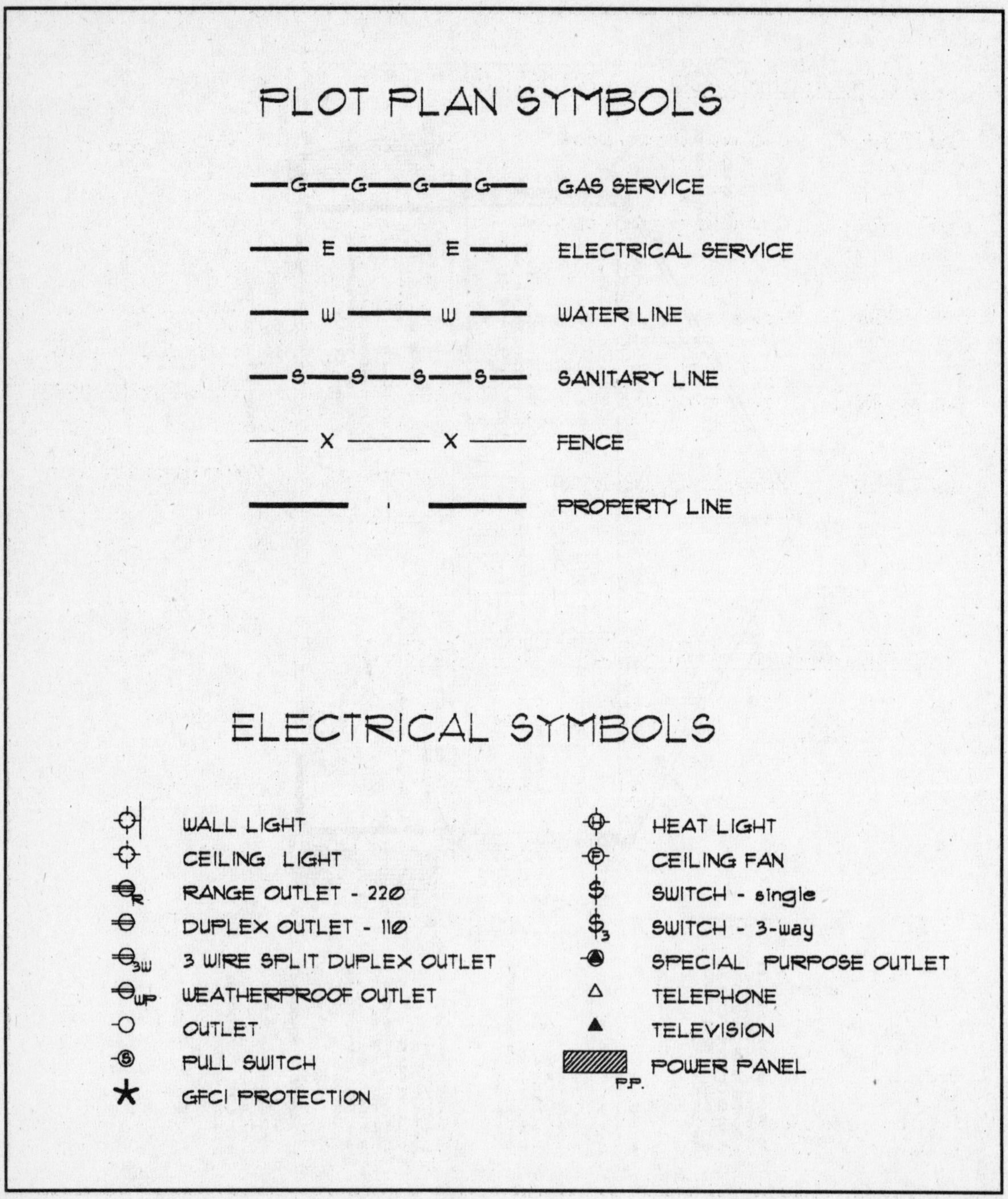

PLOT PLAN SYMBOLS

—G——G——G——G—— GAS SERVICE

——E——E—— ELECTRICAL SERVICE

——W——W—— WATER LINE

—S——S——S——S— SANITARY LINE

——X——X—— FENCE

——·—— PROPERTY LINE

ELECTRICAL SYMBOLS

⊖⊢	WALL LIGHT	⊕	HEAT LIGHT
⊖	CEILING LIGHT	Ⓕ	CEILING FAN
⊖R	RANGE OUTLET - 220	$	SWITCH - single
⊖	DUPLEX OUTLET - 110	$3	SWITCH - 3-way
⊖3W	3 WIRE SPLIT DUPLEX OUTLET	⊖	SPECIAL PURPOSE OUTLET
⊖WP	WEATHERPROOF OUTLET	△	TELEPHONE
○	OUTLET	▲	TELEVISION
⊖S	PULL SWITCH	▨ (P.P.)	POWER PANEL
✶	GFCI PROTECTION		

FIGURE #18
DOOR, WINDOW, APPLIANCE, AND FIXTURE SYMBOLS

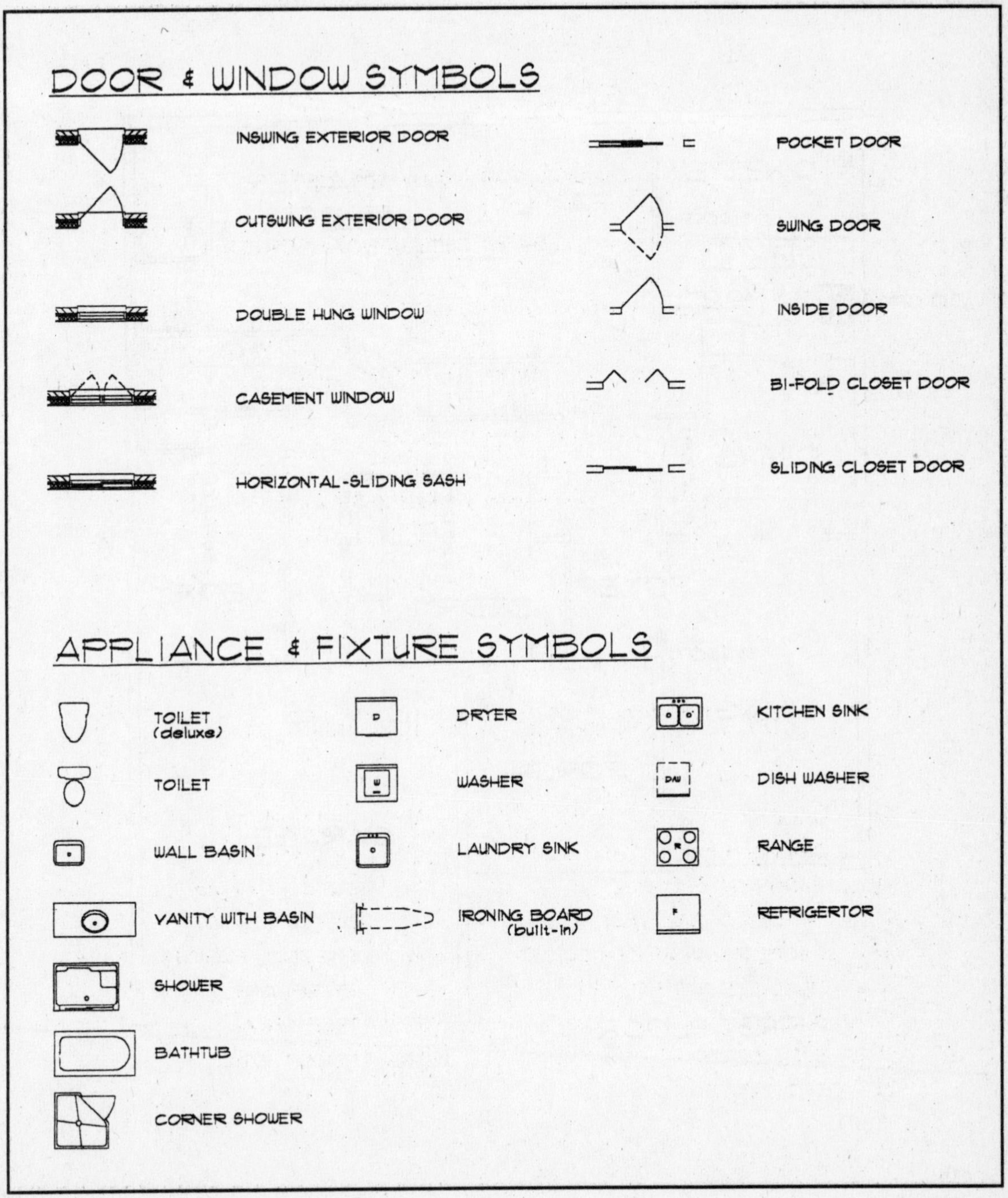

DOOR & WINDOW SYMBOLS

INSWING EXTERIOR DOOR	POCKET DOOR
OUTSWING EXTERIOR DOOR	SWING DOOR
DOUBLE HUNG WINDOW	INSIDE DOOR
CASEMENT WINDOW	BI-FOLD CLOSET DOOR
HORIZONTAL-SLIDING SASH	SLIDING CLOSET DOOR

APPLIANCE & FIXTURE SYMBOLS

TOILET (deluxe)	DRYER	KITCHEN SINK
TOILET	WASHER	DISH WASHER
WALL BASIN	LAUNDRY SINK	RANGE
VANITY WITH BASIN	IRONING BOARD (built-in)	REFRIGERTOR
SHOWER		
BATHTUB		
CORNER SHOWER		

FIGURE #19
HEATING LAYOUT

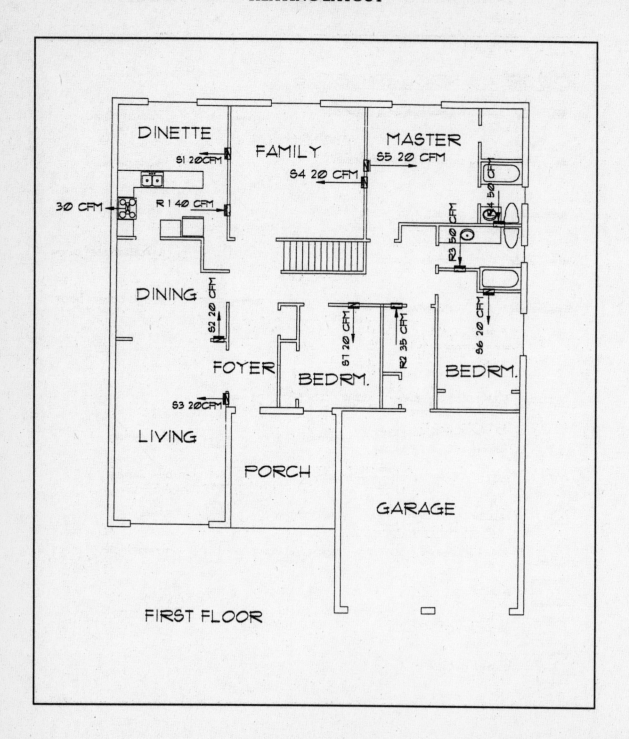

FIRST FLOOR

FIGURE #19 — Continued

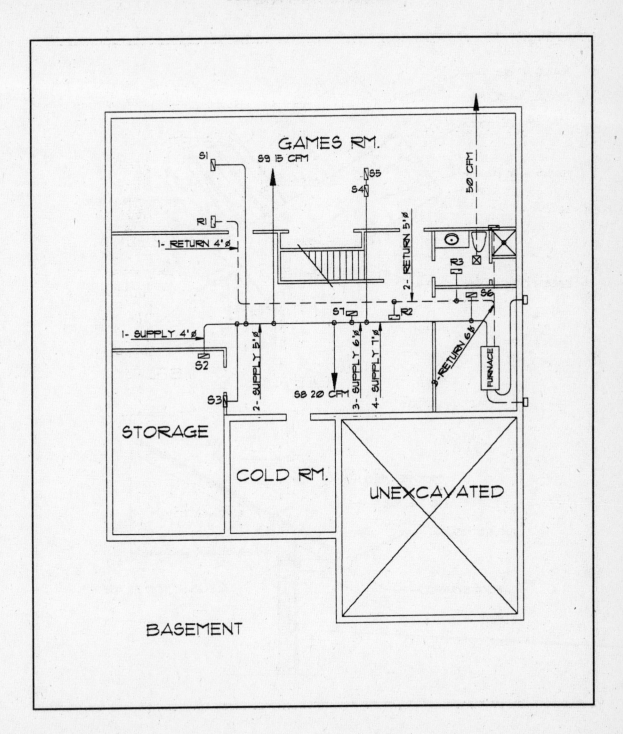

FIGURE #20
ROOF TRUSS PLAN

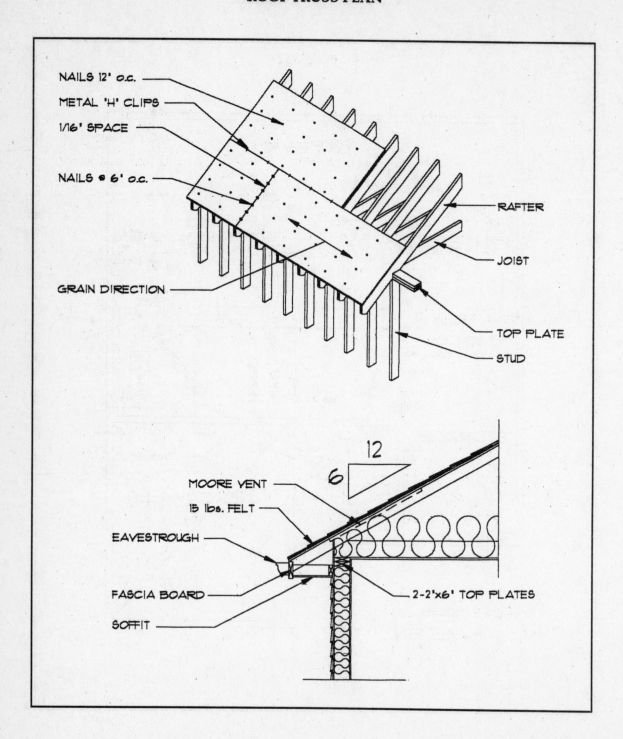

NAILS 12' o.c.

METAL 'H' CLIPS

1/16' SPACE

NAILS @ 6' o.c.

GRAIN DIRECTION

RAFTER

JOIST

TOP PLATE

STUD

12
6

MOORE VENT

15 lbs. FELT

EAVESTROUGH

FASCIA BOARD

SOFFIT

2-2'x6' TOP PLATES

FIGURE #21
TRUSS COMPONENTS

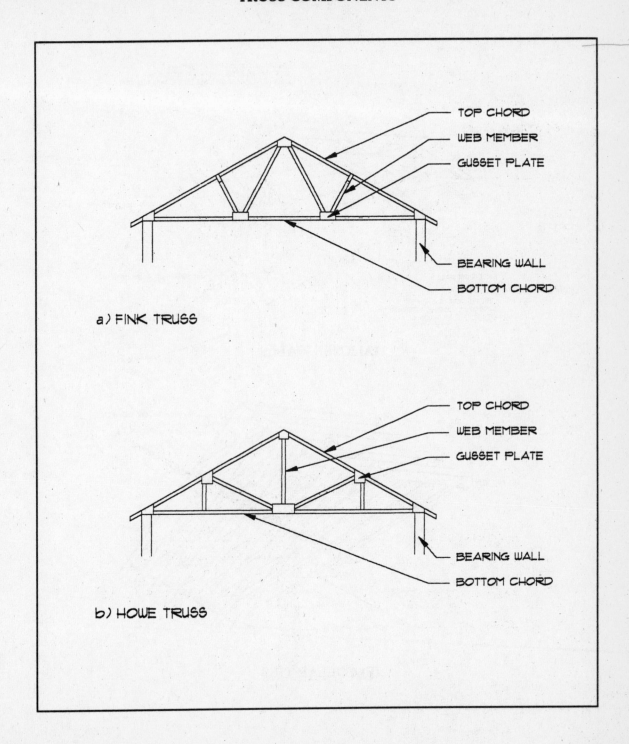

TOP CHORD
WEB MEMBER
GUSSET PLATE
BEARING WALL
BOTTOM CHORD

a) FINK TRUSS

TOP CHORD
WEB MEMBER
GUSSET PLATE
BEARING WALL
BOTTOM CHORD

b) HOWE TRUSS

FIGURE #22
RAFTER SYSTEM

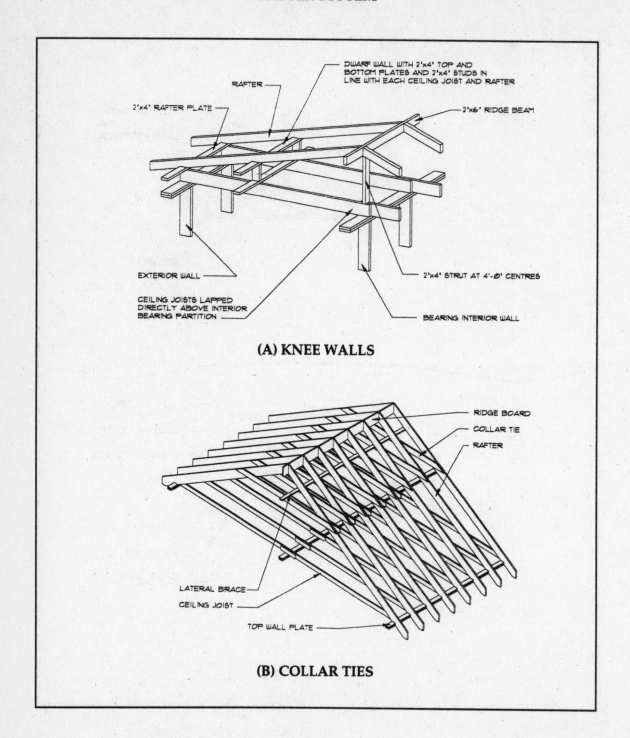

DWARF WALL WITH 2'x4' TOP AND BOTTOM PLATES AND 2'x4' STUDS IN LINE WITH EACH CEILING JOIST AND RAFTER

RAFTER

2'x4' RAFTER PLATE

2'x6' RIDGE BEAM

EXTERIOR WALL

2'x4' STRUT AT 4'-0' CENTRES

CEILING JOISTS LAPPED DIRECTLY ABOVE INTERIOR BEARING PARTITION

BEARING INTERIOR WALL

(A) KNEE WALLS

RIDGE BOARD

COLLAR TIE

RAFTER

LATERAL BRACE

CEILING JOIST

TOP WALL PLATE

(B) COLLAR TIES

FIGURE #23
LOT GRADING

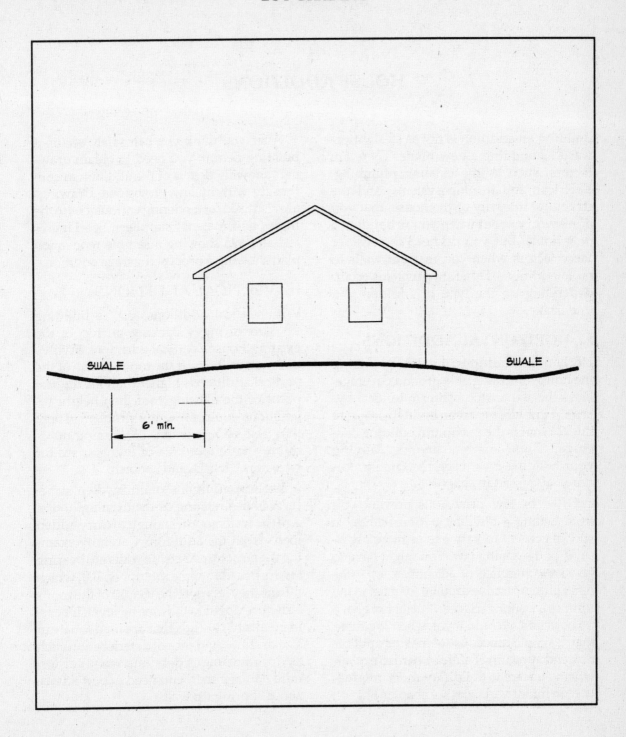

8
HOUSE ADDITIONS

Building an addition is not as straightforward as building a new home. There are factors, such as the existing plumbing, electrical, and heating systems, and the structural integrity of the house, that you don't worry about when you're building a new home. But you do need to consider these factors when you tear out walls to build additions. Different problems occur, depending on the type of addition you undertake.

a. HORIZONTAL ADDITIONS

Horizontal additions involve spreading the house onto available ground coverage. Does this expansion conform to local by-laws? How close can you build to property lines? What is the maximum building coverage? These answers involve defining your building area using the same procedures discussed in chapter 3.

Often by-law provisions prevent you from getting a building permit without a special consent to vary one or more provisions of the zoning law. You might have to go to a committee of adjustment or some other administrative tribunal for relief in the form of a minor variance. If neighbors have no objection, it could involve nothing more than a simple procedure of making application and appearing before a board to explain what you want to build. (For more information on minor variances see chapter 14.)

After you think you can safely secure a building permit, you need to obtain drawings showing details of the addition in conformity with by-law provisions. Drawings are also used for tendering various jobs to the trades and material suppliers. See Figures #24 and #25 showing a sample renovation plan showing a proposed garage addition.

b. VERTICAL ADDITIONS

With vertical additions, you're building up, sort of piggy backing on top of the existing house. Vertical additions involve different by-laws. If the top roof line of the vertical addition is higher than the highest point of the existing roof then height restrictions could present a problem. There may also be restrictions concerning maximum square foot area of living space for two-storey levels, and so forth.

Vertical additions often involve structural issues relating to the existing house. Are the walls sound enough to carry added loads from the addition? Carefully examine the structure. Outside walls are bearing (as are possibly some interior walls), which means they support the weight of the roof's structure down to the footing level. If bearing walls have studs that are inadequate in size or show evidence of deterioration such as dry rot (fungus decaying wood) or termite damage then you need expert advice about shoring up walls.

Defective walls will show signs of bowing, buckling, or sagging, and often windows are difficult to open. Place a level on the floor areas to see if they are out of level. Check for foundation cracks that suggest either inadequate bearing soil causing a weight shift or unsuitable foundation material for bearing the existing structure's weight.

Make a careful examination, but exercise caution by getting a second opinion from an expert. Call an experienced renovator or structural engineer with technical know-how. They can give you valuable advice on these matters and determine what remedial action is necessary for shoring-up any structural deficiency.

c. ORIENTATE FOR SOLAR EFFECT

Determine how the sun's rays strike the window openings of the new addition. What affect does the addition have on adjoining rooms? Will those areas be brighter or darker as a result of the addition? (See Figure #11 in chapter 5.) See how the sun's rays affect the proposed addition as it passes over your property. Keep in mind window sizes and the direction windows will face.

d. BLEND WITH THE EXISTING STYLE

How many times have you taken notice of additions that look like dreadful afterthoughts? They look as if someone took a shed and moved it against the house. Take extra time and effort to plan a pleasing style, one that blends or complements the home. The investment you're making in time and materials could be lost by poor design.

Select styles and designs that complement or blend with what already exists. A pleasing appearance enhances value. Sketch ideas you've seen from plan books and make photocopies; drive to different areas and observe how others construct additions; go to local lumberyards and pick up free handouts on renovation ideas. Go to the library and examine renovation books. Ask a lot of questions.

Windows and doors should match the existing house. The new exterior cladding or bricking material has to either blend or complement the home. The connection between the new and old should appear continuous as if the addition was always there.

Try building roof lines so they appear to flow with the rest of the house. Harmonization successfully blends the new with the old. Strive for something that appears to come together rather than creating two obvious divisions.

e. WHAT AFFECT DOES THE ADDITION HAVE ON EXISTING SYSTEMS?

The home operates as a complex integration of structural, electrical, heating, cooling, and plumbing subsystems. All additions affect one or more of those systems, and you need to know in advance which ones will be affected to determine the extent of the hidden costs you will incur.

It is not uncommon for the electrical, heating, and plumbing systems to need updating during a renovation. Changes to existing systems are expensive, especially the labor and materials for tearing out, replacing, and disposing of the old systems.

f. ASSESS THE EFFECT OF DIMINISHING RETURNS

Assess the financial pay back before undertaking any addition. Remember the principle of diminishing returns. Many owners sink money into a project and never recover a penny of it because they overbuilt for the area.

For example, suppose you purchased your home two years ago for $120 000 and the average selling price is from $120 000 to $127 000. If the total cost of renovations is $35 000, your total investment is $155 000, which is about $30 000 above average selling prices for your area.

If you want to sell in the near future, you might not recover a penny of your renovation investment. So before plunging into renovation plans, ask yourself what it will cost in the end. Is the investment going to have a pay back? How much do you need to get if you were to sell sometime in the near future?

Renovation jobs diminish in value under resale situations. You may need to re-think the project. Consider scaling down or look into building a new home.

But, if you've determined the hidden costs and the project makes economic sense, hire an architect or architectural draftsperson to prepare formal drawings, specifications, and perhaps a site plan. You need those building documents to tender the project to subcontractors and material suppliers and to file an application to obtain a building permit.

FIGURE #24
BUILDING LOCATION PLAN — RENOVATION

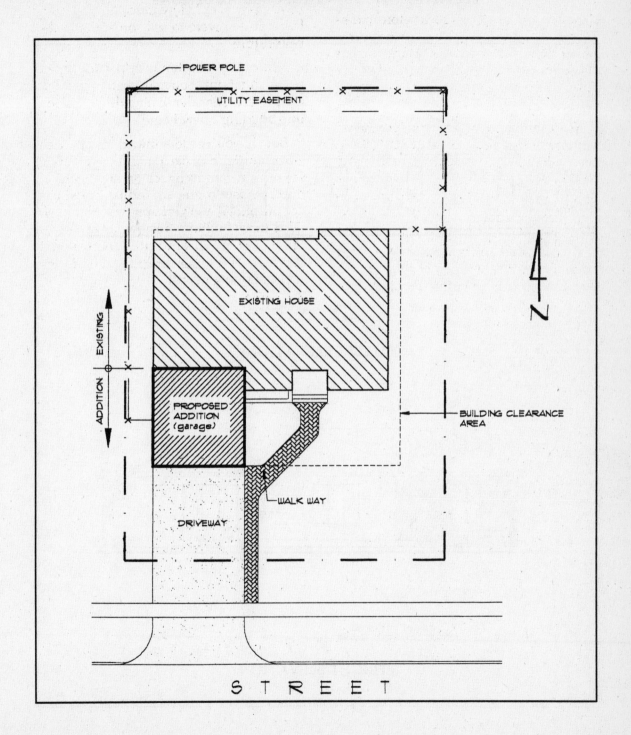

FIGURE #25
ELEVATION VIEWS — PROPOSED ADDITION

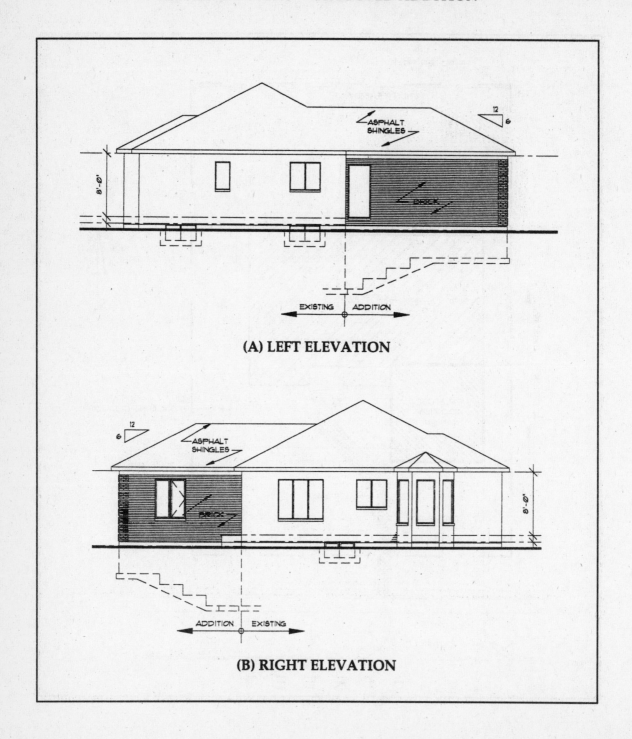

(A) LEFT ELEVATION

(B) RIGHT ELEVATION

FIGURE #25 — Continued

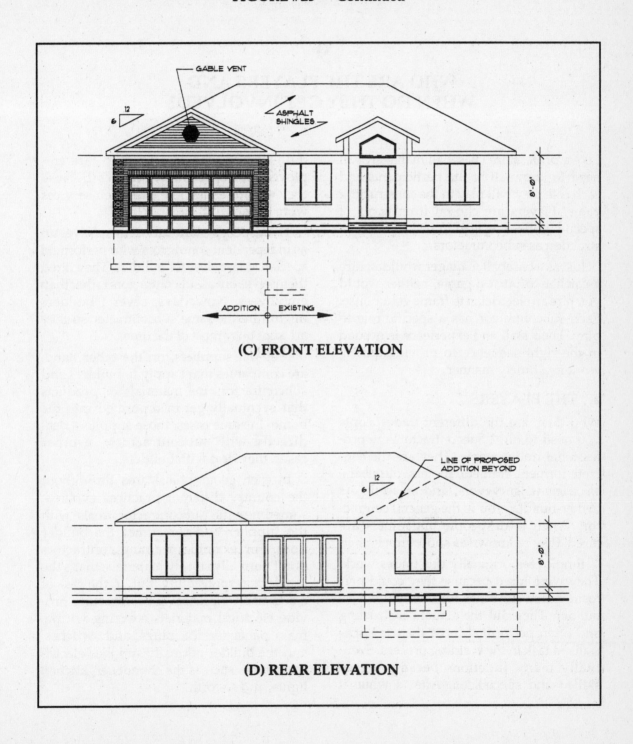

(C) FRONT ELEVATION

(D) REAR ELEVATION

9
WHO ARE THE PLAYERS AND WHEN DO THEY GET INVOLVED?

Like a professional baseball manager, you need to know all of the participants and each role they will play in the constructing game. Players are chosen from pools of specific trades engaged in residential construction as subcontractors.

Just as a baseball manager wouldn't hire a catcher to pitch a game, neither would you hire an electrician to frame your house. Each subcontractor has a specific role to play. Their skill and experience is needed in the right sequence to provide quality work in a timely manner.

a. THE PLAYERS

Who then, are the different tradespeople you need to hire? Subcontractors are professional tradespeople. They are the concrete formers, framers, roofers, plumbers, electricians, surveyors, and so forth. As owner-builder, you're the general contractor. When tradespeople and others are hired, they're known as subcontractors.

Employees originally did trades work. They were hired because they could perform varied functions for their employer-builder. They did the actual constructing and often performed more than one specialized task in the building process. Eventually many functions became highly skilled and specialized. After a while it didn't make economic sense to hire employees for specialized services because they would remain idle until their services were needed.

Tradespeople started to set themselves up as independent contractors who performed specialized services for builders. They hired themselves out as subcontractors rather than employees. Nowadays, several builders might hire the same subcontractor so they are kept busy most of the time.

Material suppliers, on the other hand, are companies that supply to builders and subcontractors the materials or products that eventually get incorporated into the home. In some cases, those suppliers deal directly with subcontractors; in other cases, they deal with builders.

In each geographical area throughout the country different practices evolved; sometimes the subcontractor deals with the supplier and sometimes the builder does. For example, framing contractors don't normally supply materials; that's the builder's responsibility. But, in the case of electricians, electrical subcontractors provide electrical materials covering wiring, main panel service, plugs, and switches, and the builder normally supplies electrical fixtures such as the chandelier, kitchen lights, and so forth.

Heating and ventilating materials are supplied by heating subcontractors. Plumbing pipes and plumbing fixtures such as tubs, sinks, toilets, and faucets are usually supplied by the plumber based on their standard fixture allowance with upgrades as an extra option for the builder.

Determine at the outset who is responsible for supplying which materials: you or the subcontractor. Then you know which suppliers you need to deal with separately. Appendix 4 indicates which material supplier will get involved with you instead of the subcontractor. But this is subject to change depending on where you live.

The next two chapters discuss strategies to deal with subcontractors and suppliers; you will appreciate how important it is to clarify responsibilities such as who is supplying materials.

Before beginning with the building steps, always remember the building inspections. Those inspectors are like umpires in a baseball game; without them you can't play. They are brought into the process at different stages, and you need their approval to get the project built.

b. THE SEQUENCE OF BUILDING STEPS

Let's begin with the sequence of building steps: the order in which you hire subcontractors to build your home. The following discussion summarizes the steps to give you an idea of the flow of work to be done. You can later refer to Appendix 2 for a reference of the participants and the sequence of their work in chart form.

In this process, you will need to fit in those suppliers you are directly involved with as the builder instead of the subcontractor; also

fit in the building inspectors who make rulings during the building stages.

The first step is to hire an excavator who grades and scrapes the topsoil and mounds it in a convenient place away from the excavation site. If the lot is without municipal water service, then a well is dug or drilled.

Next an ideal location is chosen for the house within the perimeters defined inside the building area as discussed in chapter 3.

Surveyors then stake the lot where the excavation hole is opened for footings and foundation walls. They drive several stakes into the ground and delineate the outside perimeter of the actual excavation. The stakes mark off where the excavator digs, and an elevation is provided where the depth of the excavation should ideally be located.

Normally the excavated site is about four to five feet larger than the actual area for footings and foundation walls. This gives concrete forming contractors enough room to maneuver between the walls of the excavated ground and the area where the forming for the footings and foundation walls are placed.

The excavating contractor trenches and lays in municipal water, sewer, and other services underground from the edge of the front property line to the inside of the actual excavated hole.

Excess ground dug up from excavating that isn't trucked away is mounded up and compacted beside the site. The earth forms a ramp to enable concrete trucks to climb high enough above the site to use gravity to flow concrete down a chute and into the hole where cribbing retains the concrete for footings. This cribbing is about six inches thick and 18 inches wide. It forms a solid base for foundation walls after the footing hardens and cures. Then the foundation walls sit on top.

The surveyor returns to mark off the exact location where the walls for the foundation sit on the footings. This operation ensures that the foundation walls sit in the accurate position. Depending on local practice and the specifications called for in the house plans, walls could be constructed of poured concrete, concrete block, or preserved wood.

Figure #26 shows three types of foundation walls. The type specified dictates the type of subcontractor you select to construct the walls: a framing subcontractor for wood, a concrete former for poured concrete, and a block layer for concrete block walls. The foundation walls are then dampproofed. See Figure #27 for an illustration.

Weeping tile and gravel is placed around the outside perimeter of the foundation walls. In some provinces the building code requires a type of water shield (commonly referred to as a drainage layer). This is wrapped around the foundation perimeter after the dampproofing dries.

Gravel is placed on the inside of the foundation walls to build it up so that it's level with the top of the footings. Normally this work is performed by concrete formers.

Weeping tile is designed to permit water and moisture to flow away, acting as a drainage system. It prevents water from building up against the foundation walls; otherwise, it would eventually penetrate and cause a leaky basement. Figure #28 illustrates a foundation drainage tile plan.

After the building department approves the work, the excavating subcontractor

gets the go ahead to backfill and close in the drainage system. Mounded excess material that was ramped beside the excavation site is pushed into the cavity between the ground wall and the walls of the foundation until it is filled to rough grade level. Foundation walls now act as a retaining wall for the earth. The foundation also acts as the main bearing for the framing structure.

If there is no public sewage available, a private system consisting of a septic tank, a distribution box, and a field absorption bed (see Figure #29) is installed on the lot.

A contractor specializing in private sewage systems is hired. They take out the permit from the public health department or some other environmental agency. After the sewage system is installed, framers can commence framing the house.

Framing materials are delivered in loads. Normally the framer ensures that lumber loads are delivered on time. Coordinating delivery is initially the responsibility of the builder, so it is important for you to assign that function to the lumberyard salesperson and the framer.

The first lumber load is sent, which is the deck load. It consists of wooden beams, basement lumber, interior bearing walls (if any), and decking material to cap over the foundation which constitutes the first floor level (see Figure #30).

If steel beams are specified instead of wood bearing walls or girders, then a steel fabricator makes up custom-sized beams and delivers them to the site. The beams sit into pockets provided in the foundation walls before decking material is capped on top.

The remaining lumber loads are delivered as they are needed. The framer keeps in close touch with the lumber supplier and ensures that each additional load is delivered on time. See Figure #31, which shows wall framing sections.

Note: Make sure your framer sets aside defective materials for the lumberyard to pick up and credit to your account.

Depending on the roof structure proposed — roof rafters or roof trusses — the framer builds the roof either by hand using lumber pieces for rafters, collar ties, and knee walls (see Figure #22 in chapter 7) or roof trusses may be built off-site by a roof truss manufacturer. Refer back to Figure #21 in chapter 7 showing samples of two types of fabricated trusses that are engineered to building specifications.

Windows and doors are supplied through lumberyards yet are more often ordered directly from window and door manufacturers. Select from several manufacturers; compare for price and quality.

Take time to meet with at least one window and door sales representative. Learn from them; this will help you find the best type, size, and quality of window to select. Window and door quotations are similar between manufacturers. Their quotes list the window and door opening sizes and the type and quality of the windows and doors. Compare all the quoted prices. (The next chapter discusses a method for choosing the best quotes from subcontractors and material suppliers.)

When the framing is complete with windows and doors installed, order a building inspection for the framing work. Wait until approval is received before starting the rest of the interior work.

While waiting, arrange a meeting with the kitchen cupboard supplier. They will come to the site and mark out the location of the cupboards and vanities. Use a black felt pen and mark the exact location for electrical boxes and plumbing connections or any deviations from the plans.

After the framing is approved, go ahead with the rough-ins. Rough-ins are part of the mechanical equipment that is installed between the walls. Begin with the plumber who installs the underground pipes in the basement. Then have them install the above-ground plumbing. At the same time, arrange for the roofer to install shingles and flashing, but don't forget to order roofing materials before they arrive to cover the roof.

When the plumbing is roughed in, the plumber will immediately order a plumbing inspection, and if it's approved, the concrete floor finisher can place concrete on the basement floor. At the same time, the concrete finishers can pour the garage floors. After a few days the concrete hardens and cures to permit trades to walk on it.

Next, rough in the heating and ventilation by having the subcontractor install the furnace and ducting. When they finish, they will order a heating and ventilation inspection.

The electrician follows the heating and ventilating subcontractor. This is the last major rough-in to install. A service panel and wires are roughed in. Then the electrician orders an electrical rough-in inspection.

Note: At this stage after the wiring is roughed in, make sure all inspections covering the work to this stage are finalized and approved before proceeding with other interior work.

While waiting, you can arrange to have the painter prime paint the outside. Then the masonry or siding subcontractor can start covering outside walls. Exterior cladding or masonry veneer materials are ordered from suppliers. Figure #32 illustrates different exterior coverings.

In the case of masonry, such as brick, those material suppliers will measure up the quantity and deliver the materials you need. A salesperson will either arrive at your site to measure directly or will use your plans and specifications.

With siding materials, either the installer or material supplier measures the amount of materials needed to cover with exterior cladding.

When a brick chimney is proposed, make sure flashing details (see Glossary) are properly installed between the roof and chimney. This work is arranged as soon as possible to avoid potential water damage. Figure #33 illustrates these flashing details.

After the interior inspections are complete, go ahead with the rest of the rough-ins like the phone, cable, security, central vacuuming, and intercom. Personally conduct a physical inspection of the premises to ensure that outlets, electrical boxes, and switches are in their proper place.

Now arrange for insulating the walls and ceilings (see Figure #34). Cavities between the inside and the outside framing structure are filled with insulation batts. Make sure they are laid fluffy, not cramped or squashed.

Note: If blown insulation is used in the attic then installation in that area doesn't take place until after the ceilings are boarded.

Next, arrange to cover the inside ceilings and walls with a poly vapor barrier, which is stapled to stud walls and ceiling joists to prevent air leakage and moisture damage.

After the insulation and vapor barrier is installed, order an inspection before closing in the walls with boarding material.

When the work is approved by the building inspector, order the boarding subcontractors to board interior walls and ceilings. Materials are supplied by subcontractors or by builders.

As soon as walls and ceilings are boarded, they are prepared with plastering compound material or drywall filler. After boarding and surface finishing (and sometimes texture spraying), the interior walls and ceilings are ready for painting.

Note: Texture spray is never applied to kitchens or bathroom ceilings.

Siding or stucco on the outside exterior walls is started and if a fireplace is planned, the interior masonry is finished. Next arrange for a trimming supplier to measure for baseboard, window trim, interior doors, fancy finishes, shelving, and hardware.

The painter starts on the walls and ceilings, and stains trim material, if natural woodwork is selected. The painter might supply the materials; it depends on local practice, so find out.

Carpet and tile suppliers now install resilient or ceramic floor covering over the kitchen, bathrooms, and foyer entryways. Ceramic or similar products are also applied to wall surfaces surrounding tubs, showers, and other bathroom areas.

Next is the installation of kitchen cupboards, countertops, and vanities. The kitchen cupboard supplier generally does the installation. It is best for them to cut sink openings so you need templates from the plumber for the configuration and size of the openings.

After cupboards and vanities, the trimmer starts with interior finishes by trimming-out the house. The stair supplier (or trimmer) installs railings.

When the trim and stair railings are finished the painter comes back to complete the inside (usually three coats in total). After finishing, they don't return again until just before you're ready to move in.

The interior is now ready for the systems, starting with the plumber. But you first need to arrange for the delivery of the water heater and built-in appliances.

The plumber brings the remaining fixtures like the sinks and the taps. They connect pipes for water supply, water heater, built-ins (washer, garburator, etc.), and eventually turn on the water connection.

The electrician then comes to take care of wiring and connect the service panel, furnace, thermostat, air conditioning, built-in appliances, plugs, switches, and covers. Electrical fixtures are delivered to the site before the electricians arrive. Make sure electrical fixtures are properly labelled, marked, or tagged to show exactly where in what room they are supposed to be installed.

Next, the heating and ventilating subcontractor completes piping, connects the air conditioning and furnace, and installs ducting covers. Then the systems are checked and started to ensure that they are functioning properly.

Outside on the exterior grounds, the excavator finishes grading. If a grading plan is available, the lot is staked with elevation grades at various locations instructing the grader where and how much to cut or fill areas to slope and shape the lot for draining purposes. Top soil is then placed on top of areas designated for grass and gravel on areas where driveway and walkways are planned.

A grading plan primarily designates where surface water is to be directed using a slope from the foundation and other sloping or swaling to prevent ponding or flooding the surrounding area.

The surveyor returns again to see if the new grading is in compliance with the elevations they set. Figure #35 shows typical elevation grades. Arrows show the direction to slope or swale the land.

The municipality receives a certificate prepared by the surveyor certifying that the lot is graded in compliance with the grading plan or good drainage practice. The grading certificate is filed with the building department and without it you may not be able to secure an occupancy permit.

After grading, the driveway subcontractor installs the surface covering for the driveway and walkways which might be asphalt, concrete, brick, stone, or some other material depending on what you specify. Then sod or seeding is applied to the remaining areas.

Back in the interior, the rest of the remaining rough-ins such as cable, phone, central vacuuming, intercom, and security are finished.

Next are the unfinished floors, starting first with hardwood. Carpet flooring is left for last. Then the trimmer returns to install mirrors, doors, and hardware.

The home is cleaned after the painter touches up scratched or damaged areas. Finally, you're ready for occupancy. A final inspection is ordered, which paves the way for issuance of a certificate of occupancy.

Now you have a suggested order for involving the participants who are responsible for the different aspects of the building process. Use Appendix 2 as your guide for identifying the steps in the building process.

To help with the task of directing the building process, flow charts accompanying each phase are provided in chapters 15 through to 19 and in the appendixes. Those steps will be discussed again as you proceed through the building process.

As you read through the various steps, it probably occurred to you that one of your primary functions is contracting with subcontractors and suppliers in addition to coordinating the sequence of each participant's involvement. The contracting process is what building is all about. The next few chapters show you the rules for obtaining quotes and how to turn them into written contracts, so read on.

FIGURE #26
TYPES OF FOUNDATION WALLS

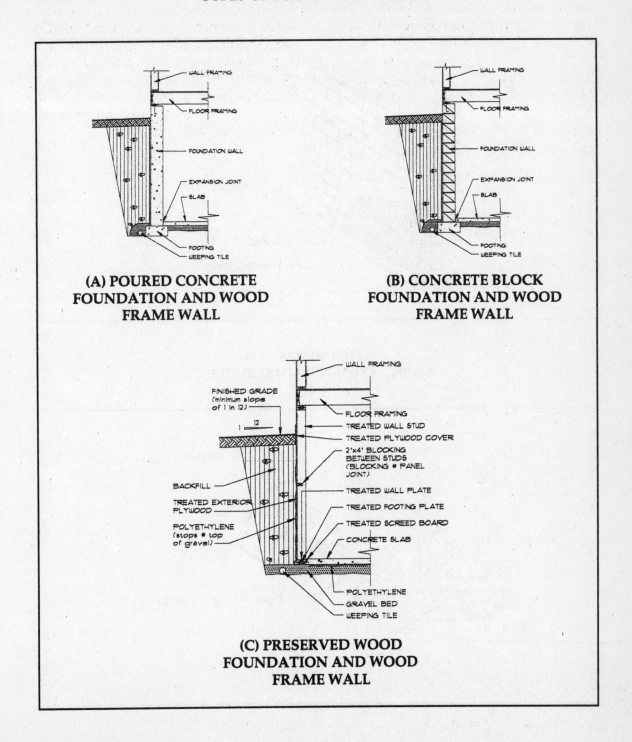

(A) POURED CONCRETE FOUNDATION AND WOOD FRAME WALL

(B) CONCRETE BLOCK FOUNDATION AND WOOD FRAME WALL

(C) PRESERVED WOOD FOUNDATION AND WOOD FRAME WALL

FIGURE #27
DAMPPROOFING FOUNDATION

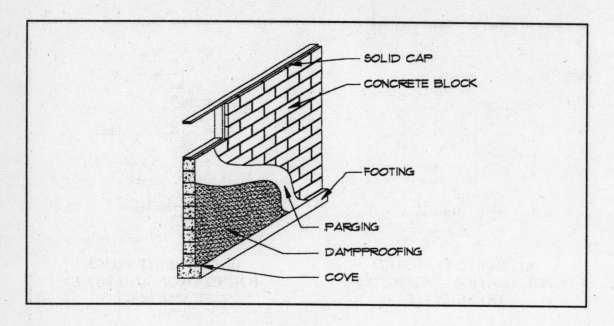

FIGURE #28
FOUNDATION DRAINAGE TILE

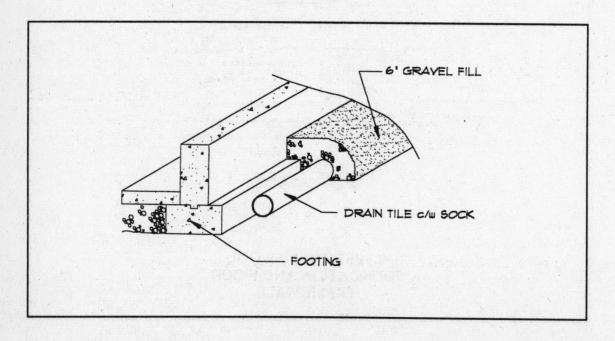

FIGURE #29
SEPTIC SYSTEM LOCATION

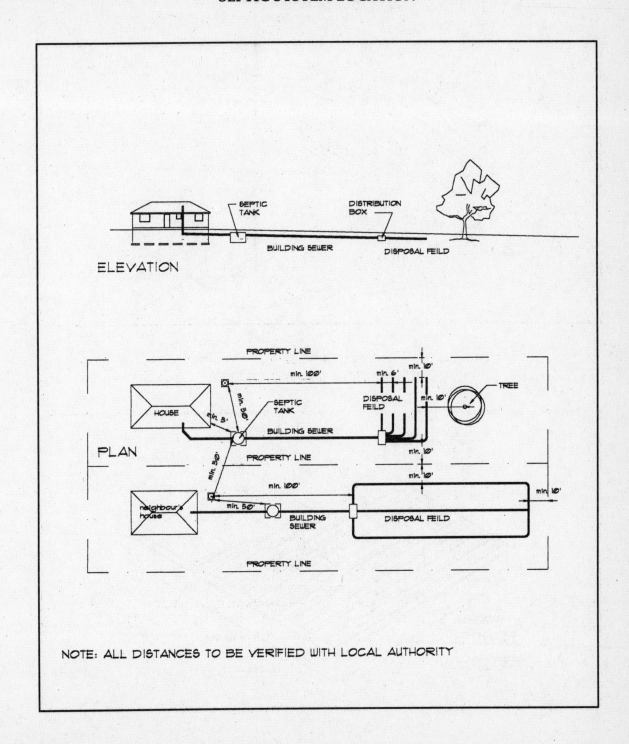

NOTE: ALL DISTANCES TO BE VERIFIED WITH LOCAL AUTHORITY

FIGURE #30
FRAMING DECK LOAD

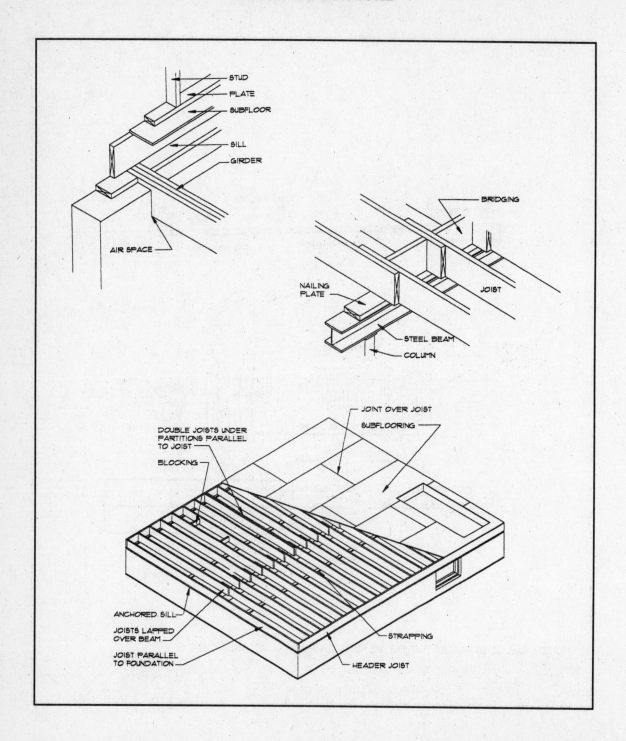

STUD

PLATE

SUBFLOOR

SILL

GIRDER

AIR SPACE

BRIDGING

JOIST

NAILING PLATE

STEEL BEAM

COLUMN

JOINT OVER JOIST

SUBFLOORING

DOUBLE JOISTS UNDER PARTITIONS PARALLEL TO JOIST

BLOCKING

ANCHORED SILL

JOISTS LAPPED OVER BEAM

JOIST PARALLEL TO FOUNDATION

STRAPPING

HEADER JOIST

FIGURE #31
FRAMING AROUND EXTERIOR WALL OPENINGS

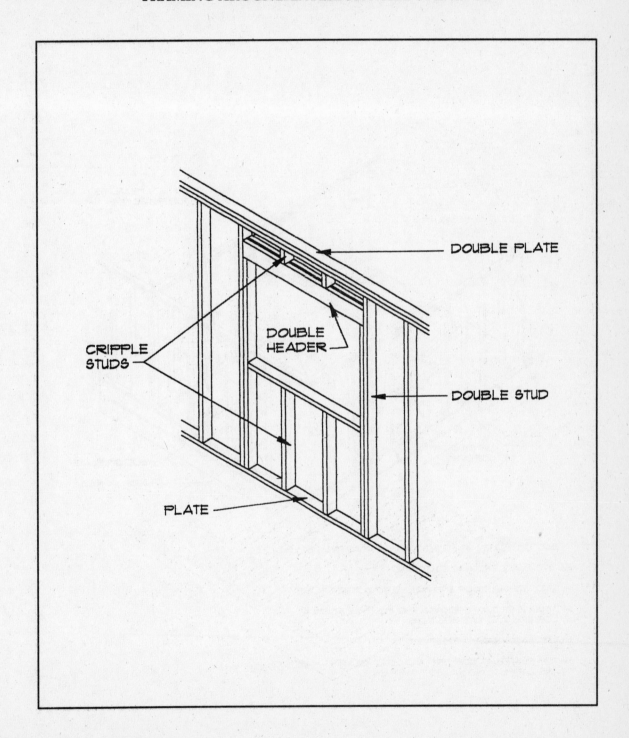

DOUBLE PLATE

DOUBLE HEADER

CRIPPLE STUDS

DOUBLE STUD

PLATE

FIGURE #31 — Continued

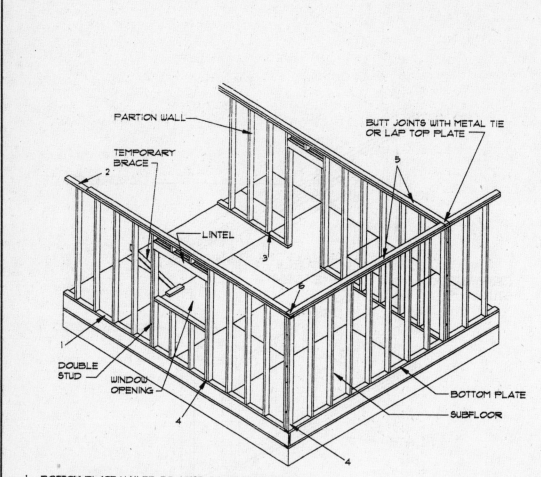

1 - BOTTOM PLATE NAILED TO JOIST OR HEADER JOIST

2 - TOP PLATE END-NAILED TO STUD

3- STUD TOENAILED OR END-NAILED TO BOTTOM PLATE

4- DOUBLE STUD AT OPENINGS AND MULTIPLE STUDS AT CORNERS AND INTERSECTIONS

5- TOP PATES NAILED TOGETHER

6- TOP PLATES AT CORNERS AND LOAD-BEARING PARTIONS ARE LAPPED AND NAILED TOGETHER

FIGURE #32
EXTERIOR COVERINGS

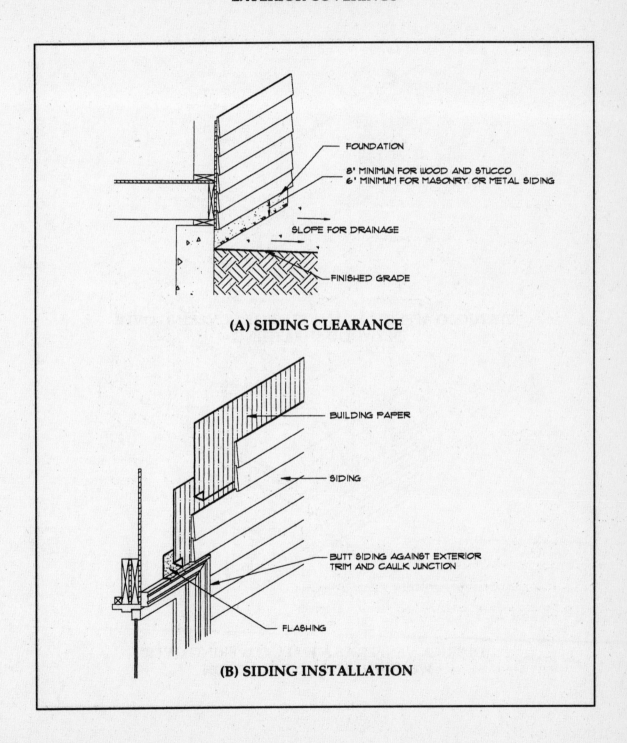

FOUNDATION

8' MINIMUN FOR WOOD AND STUCCO
6' MINIMUM FOR MASONRY OR METAL SIDING

SLOPE FOR DRAINAGE

FINISHED GRADE

(A) SIDING CLEARANCE

BUILDING PAPER

SIDING

BUTT SIDING AGAINST EXTERIOR
TRIM AND CAULK JUNCTION

FLASHING

(B) SIDING INSTALLATION

FIGURE #32 — Continued

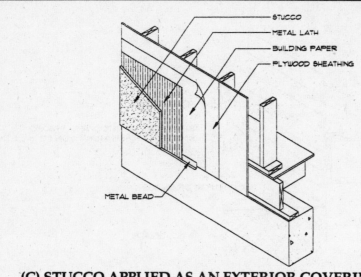

STUCCO
METAL LATH
BUILDING PAPER
PLYWOOD SHEATHING

METAL BEAD

(C) STUCCO APPLIED AS AN EXTERIOR COVERING OVER PLYWOOD SHEATHING

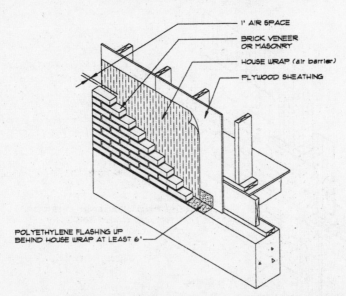

1' AIR SPACE
BRICK VENEER OR MASONRY
HOUSE WRAP (air barrier)
PLYWOOD SHEATHING

POLYETHYLENE FLASHING UP
BEHIND HOUSE WRAP AT LEAST 6'

(D) BRICK VENEER AS A WALL COVERING OVER WOOD-FRAME CONSTRUCTION

FIGURE #33
FLASHING

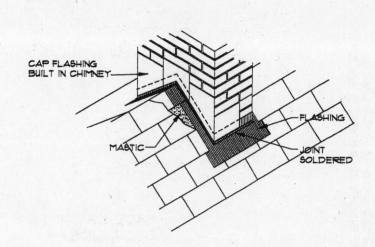

CAP FLASHING
BUILT IN CHIMNEY

MASTIC

FLASHING

JOINT
SOLDERED

(A) FLASHING AT A CHIMNEY LOCATION ON RIDGE

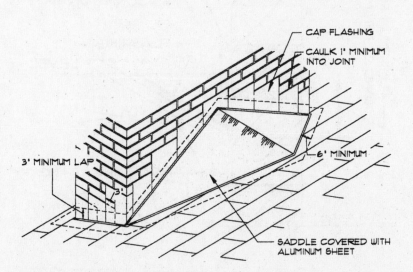

CAP FLASHING

CAULK 1' MINIMUM
INTO JOINT

3' MINIMUM LAP

6' MINIMUM

SADDLE COVERED WITH
ALUMINUM SHEET

(B) FLASHING A CHIMNEY THAT PROJECTS THROUGH
A SLOPING ROOF

FIGURE #33 — Continued

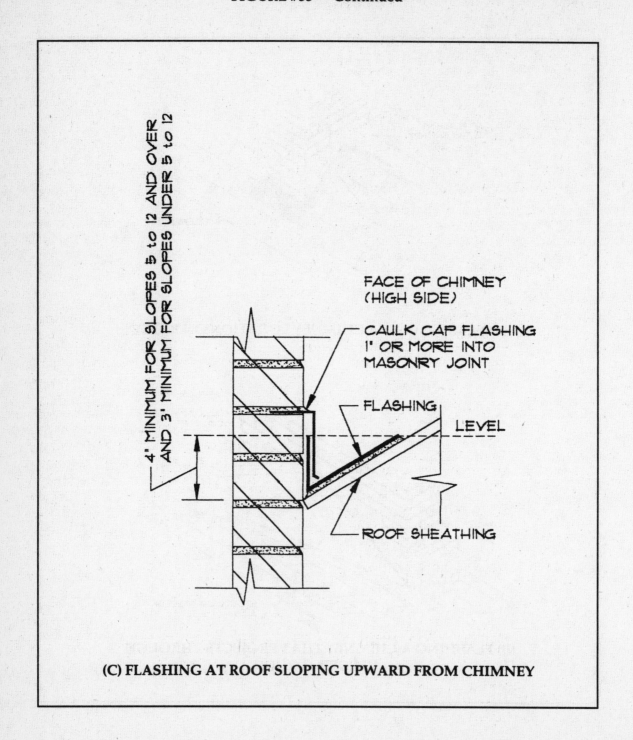

(C) FLASHING AT ROOF SLOPING UPWARD FROM CHIMNEY

FIGURE #34
INSULATION INSTALLATION

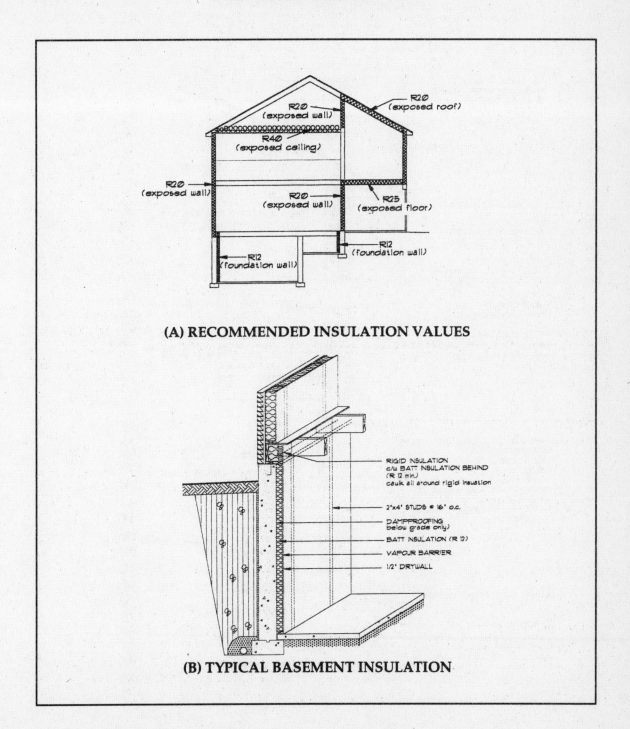

(A) RECOMMENDED INSULATION VALUES

(B) TYPICAL BASEMENT INSULATION

FIGURE #34 — Continued

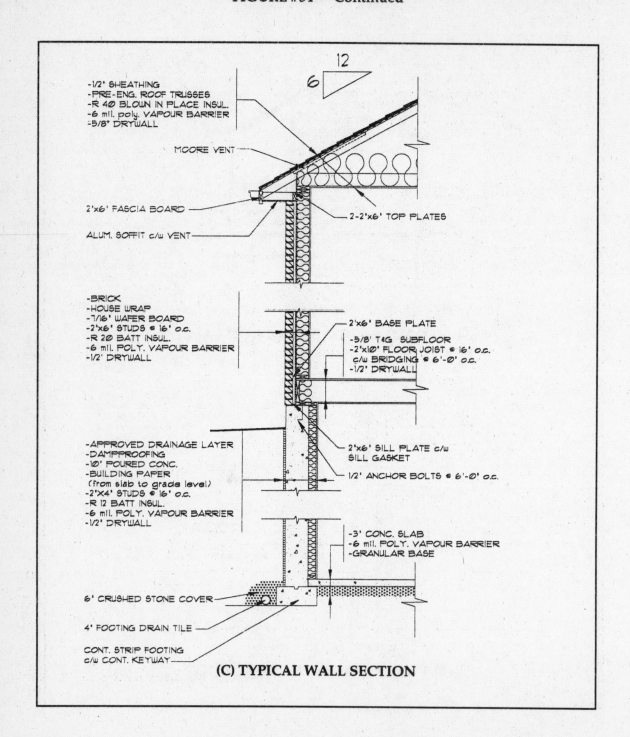

-1/2' SHEATHING
-PRE-ENG. ROOF TRUSSES
-R 40 BLOWN IN PLACE INSUL.
-6 mil. poly. VAPOUR BARRIER
-5/8" DRYWALL

12
6

MOORE VENT

2'x6' FASCIA BOARD

ALUM. SOFFIT c/w VENT

2-2'x6' TOP PLATES

-BRICK
-HOUSE WRAP
-7/16' WAFER BOARD
-2'x6' STUDS @ 16' o.c.
-R 20 BATT INSUL.
-6 mil. POLY. VAPOUR BARRIER
-1/2' DRYWALL

2'x6' BASE PLATE
-5/8' T&G SUBFLOOR
-2'x10' FLOOR JOIST @ 16' o.c.
c/w BRIDGING @ 6'-0' o.c.
-1/2' DRYWALL

-APPROVED DRAINAGE LAYER
-DAMPPROOFING
-10' POURED CONC.
-BUILDING PAPER
(from slab to grade level)
-2'X4' STUDS @ 16' o.c.
-R 12 BATT INSUL.
-6 mil. POLY. VAPOUR BARRIER
-1/2' DRYWALL

2'x6' SILL PLATE c/w
SILL GASKET

1/2' ANCHOR BOLTS @ 6'-0' o.c.

-3' CONC. SLAB
-6 mil. POLY. VAPOUR BARRIER
-GRANULAR BASE

6' CRUSHED STONE COVER

4' FOOTING DRAIN TILE

CONT. STRIP FOOTING
c/w CONT. KEYWAY

(C) TYPICAL WALL SECTION

FIGURE #35
LOT GRADING PLAN

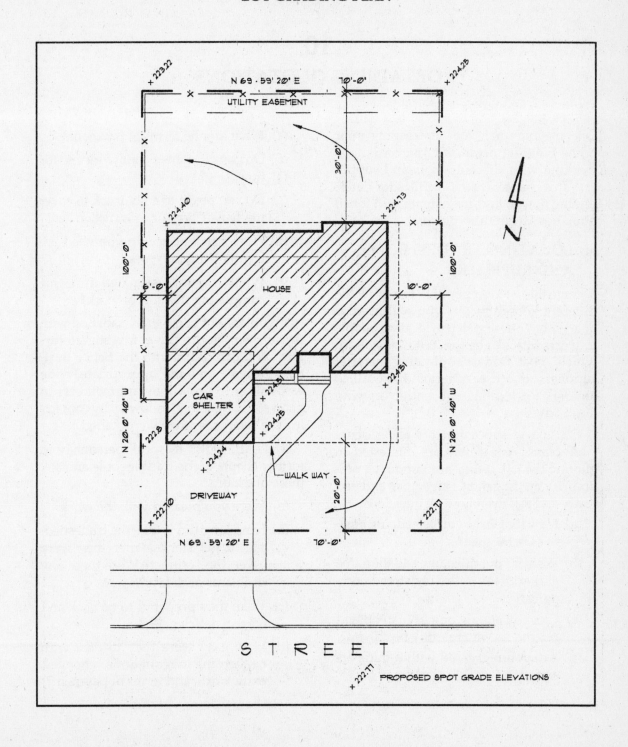

PROPOSED SPOT GRADE ELEVATIONS

10

OBTAINING QUOTATIONS

One of your main jobs in keeping your home building organized and on time is working with subcontractors and suppliers. This chapter discusses rules for determining how to find, investigate, and solicit quotations from these players.

a. LOCATING TRADESPEOPLE AND SUPPLIERS

Refer to the list in Appendix 2 to review the different subcontractors you will need to deal with. Your first step in locating people to work with can be the Yellow Pages, in which most tradespeople and material suppliers advertise. You should also talk to builders for locating subcontractors who don't advertise.

Call a few subcontractors and discuss your plans. Ask if they are interested in quoting the job. If they are, conduct a preliminary investigation. Have a pen and pad ready and ask the following questions:

(a) How long have you been doing business in the area?

(b) What is your full name and the name and address of the registered company?

(c) Can you supply names of people as references who recently hired you?

(d) Are you registered with a trade association?

(e) What are the terms of payment?

(f) Do you guarantee your work and for how long?

(g) Do you object to a holdback to cover mechanics' liens or construction liens?

(h) How much notice do you need before starting the work?

(i) What is your estimated time for completing this sort of work?

If you are not completely satisfied with the answers you receive, investigate further. You can check with the Better Business Bureau and the appropriate trade association to see if they are members in good standing. If not, follow up by contacting the references they've provided.

Make it a point to speak personally to former clients of the tradespeople and ask these questions:

(a) Were you pleased with the work?

(b) How long did it take the tradespeople to get started after they were given the contract? Were there any problems or delays?

(c) Were they prepared to go back and correct deficiencies?

(d) How easy were they to deal with concerning negotiations, changes, extra work, and terms of payment?

quotations for each aspect of the work, including the building material suppliers.

b. SOLICITING QUOTATIONS

When soliciting quotations, you are in essence formally or informally asking for a price to do a job or to deliver materials or appliances which eventually forms part of the house.

Your request for a quote might be written or verbal. Written invitations are best because you identify what you want and the conditions forming part of the contract are laid out. For this procedure to work best, you must be consistent; clearly identify what you want, so later you can compare quotations to determine which are best. Remember, they need to see your house plans and in some cases the building location plan before they can quote.

Invitation forms for inviting sub-trades and material suppliers to provide you with quotes are supplied in Appendixes 3 and 4.

1. Giving the contract to the lowest bidder

As a rule, tradespeople and material suppliers who submit the best quotation receive the contract; it's usually the one with the lowest price, all other things being equal. Of course, you should be satisfied that they have the technical know-how and experience with a record of delivering on time.

2. Paying money up front

Generally, you should never have to pay money up front. However, you must consider if the request is justified, as in some cases the request may be reasonable. For example, a third party such as a manufacturer may be hired for fabricating or making up a specialized item to fulfill the subcontractor's contract responsibilities, and in turn has to pay a deposit up front. In this case, a deposit is probably justified.

Such cases are rare, and if you have to pay, make the cheque payable jointly to both subcontractor and manufacturer.

3. Progress advances

Progress advances are almost never paid since it's difficult to hire someone else to finish work started by others who may possibly quit or abandon the work.

Some tradespeople now ask for an advance at the rough-in stage. Electricians and plumbers particularly are notorious for requesting this sort of payment procedure.

In situations where a draw cannot be avoided, limit the amount to no more than one-third of the contract price. Also, provide a condition that the work is inspected and approved by the appropriate inspector before payment is made.

4. Doing part of the work yourself

As a rule, you should let the subcontractors do all the work. Devote your time to finding good tradespeople, arranging contracts, scheduling, and inspecting their work. This is enough to keep you busy if you're doing a good job. Don't overwhelm yourself; if you get immersed in too much detail, you could lose money in the end.

There are exceptions to this rule, however. If you have extra time or experience in doing the jobs, then you could save labor costs by helping out. But under a deadline, play it safe; stick to being the builder.

As owner-builder you now have some rules to follow for obtaining quotes. The next chapter shows how to turn the best quotations into favorable contracts.

11

CREATING CONTRACTS AND AVOIDING PROBLEMS

Now that you've selected the best quotations from your tradespeople and suppliers, you should turn them into favorable contracts.

a. VERBAL OR WRITTEN QUOTATIONS

Most subcontractors itemize the work they agree to perform and most material suppliers itemize materials they agree to deliver by using quotation forms. These are pre-printed forms containing a few standard clauses about respective liabilities of the parties. Space is provided for both parties to sign, and when it is signed, the quotation becomes a legal enforceable contract.

Verbal agreements can also be binding. For example, suppose you receive a quotation signed by a material supplier, but you haven't signed it yourself. You simply say to the supplier, "it's all right," and the supplier delivers the materials. Legally, it makes no difference that you didn't sign the quotation. You still entered into a binding contract and the terms of the quotation define the rights and liabilities. The contract contains elements of writing and a verbal element of acceptance.

As another example, suppose you receive a signed quotation and you tell the subcontractor, "I agree to accept provided you agree to a one-year warranty."

Later the subcontractor performs the work, but nine months later there's a problem, and you call to ask them to honor the warranty. They reply, "I'm not obligated to a warranty because it's not in my quote."

What are the legal consequences? By law the subcontractor is liable for the warranty even though it isn't in writing. This is, of course, provided that the court accepts your version of what was discussed.

If another party performs knowing that acceptance was conditional on a one-year warranty, there is an implication that the warranty is a term of the contract. It represents a verbal acceptance on behalf of the subcontractor accepting your condition by implication.

However, it's difficult to prove implied terms when numerous verbal assurances and exchanges are made aside from the written quotation. It becomes difficult trying to establish later on what was agreed to between parties.

How do you ascertain which verbal representations or exchanges were intended to become terms and which were merely negotiations, never intended to be acted on? If this sort of problem goes to court, someone must interpret what the parties intended. In other words, what are the terms of the contract?

If discussions are not clearly defined or clear cut as in the two previous examples, you'll have a 50-50 chance of succeeding — against a shrewd lawyer, perhaps less than 50%.

These are good reasons to put all your terms in writing. Whenever you're not sure about some responsibility, add a written clause or term to the contract.

b. HOW TO CREATE A FAVORABLE CONTRACT

You don't need to incur huge legal fees by having your lawyer draft all your contracts. You can do much of the work yourself.

Generally, when you first receive a quotation from a subcontractor or material supplier, often you will want to add some important terms. You could employ one of four methods to ensure your terms are included. First, you can record them directly onto the quotation form. Second, you can attach a separate sheet to the form, containing your terms. Third, you can forward a covering letter of acceptance conditional on the acceptance of your itemized terms. Finally, you can create your own contract.

Use one of the methods described here, rather than doing nothing or extending verbal representations or exchanges that may have a different interpretation later on. Avoid ending up in court at the mercy of fate.

1. Record your terms directly onto the quotation form

To record your terms onto the quotation form, you could write something like this: "I accept provided...[then state your terms]." After stating the terms, date the form, sign in the place provided, make a copy, and deliver the amended form to the subcontractor or material supplier. If they perform their part

of the bargain after receiving your terms, then they've accepted them.

It is not imperative for the other party to sign again, although it makes it easier for you to prove the contract terms in court if they initial or sign where you've added terms. As an extra precaution, you might have the subcontractor or supplier initial the copy you keep as an acknowledgment of acceptance of the added terms.

2. Attach a separate sheet of paper with your terms

When there is insufficient space on the form, write "additional terms attached" somewhere on the front page of the quotation and place your initials beside those words. But don't sign the front of the quotation form. Just attach a separate sheet with your conditions, initial that sheet also, and deliver a copy of each (the quotation form and attached sheet) to the subcontractor or material supplier.

As in the previous situation, if the other side performs their part of the contract, they are bound by your additional terms even though they haven't signed or specifically agreed to it. As a precaution you could have them initial or sign on the separate sheet you keep which contains your additional terms.

3. Mail a separate covering letter with your terms

If you cannot use one of the two preceding methods after receiving a quote, add somewhere on the front of the form the following: "Additional terms attached." Don't sign the quotation in the space provided; just put your initials beside the added words.

Send a registered letter with the amended form and keep a copy of everything for yourself. In the letter indicate "I accept your quotation provided the terms outlined here [state your terms] form part of the contract." Make sure you sign the letter. If the other side verbally accepts or performs part of the contract, they are bound by your terms as outlined in the letter.

4. Create your own written contract

Sometimes you won't get a written quotation. If the subcontractor says verbally he or she will do the job for a stipulated price, or perhaps simply writes down the price for a job on a piece of letterhead, you are left without a quotation form to work from and there are no written terms itemized. In this case, you can prepare a written contract to protect yourself. (See Appendix 15 for a model agreement.)

Remember, a model contract is just a guideline for assistance. It suggests most of the terms that you will want to negotiate, but there might be other terms personal to your particular circumstances you might want to negotiate and include in the contract terms.

Written terms provide the only protection. It's a lot more difficult for lawyers to argue against black and white. When disputes do arise, the lawyer representing the subcontractor is more likely to negotiate than challenge you in court.

c. POTENTIAL PROBLEMS WHEN DEALING WITH SUBCONTRACTORS

As owner-builder, you need to avoid potential problems when hiring subcontractors and material suppliers. Although it's practically impossible to anticipate every problem, you can level the playing field if you investigate and include terms in contracts whenever you suspect a problem.

Remember, you're dealing with business people who proved they can succeed; they know what to anticipate. Prepare and protect yourself.

1. Who supplies the materials?

Always ask who supplies the materials. Does the subcontractor supply all materials? In some electrical contracts, an electrician may supply all materials except light fixtures. In other contracts, the owner-builder may supply all materials while the subcontractor only supplies tools and labor.

Make sure this point is clearly addressed in the contract. If it is not, add one of the following terms:

(a) "The owner-builder is responsible for supplying all materials," or,

(b) "The subcontractor is responsible for supplying all materials."

If the materials are to be shared between both parties, then add this clause: "The owner-builder supplies the following materials [list them], and the subcontractor supplies the following materials [list them]"

2. Scope of the work

Extent of the work to be done can be difficult to define within the contract. Subcontractors know what their work entails, but how do you know for sure you've covered all their work by definition in the contract? Use Appendix 2 to guide you in identifying the scope of work for different subcontractors and avoid being charged for extras.

By connecting the scope of work to your plans and specifications, you can overcome cumbersome definitions. Be sure to cover any building code changes that might occur but haven't been anticipated by the plans and specifications.

Consider a term similar to the following when you have concerns in this area:

"The work entails the following [see Appendix 2 for definitions] in accordance with the house plans, specifications, and site plan. The subcontractor furnishes all labor, tools, scaffolding, water, electricity, heat, machinery, and other services and supervision for carrying out the work according to the attached plans and specifications. Notwithstanding the plans and specifications, all work is to be carried out in accordance with applicable codes and laws having jurisdiction; and the price herein stated covers for such changes to comply with those laws. The subcontractor shall protect work, owner's property, and surrounding properties from damage occasioned by the construction and the completion of the work."

3. Determining price

As a rule, price is negotiated as a fixed sum. But with certain trades, this method may not be possible. Take, for example, the bricklayer. Bricklayers often base quotations on so much money per thousand brick laid. If you use such a formula method for determining price, you want to place an upper limit to avoid surprises and paying for extra charges covering every conceivable area of brick work.

Suppose you order 15 000 bricks and the quoted price is $450 per thousand brick. If 500 bricks are left over after the work is finished, then the price therefore is 14.5 x $450 = $6 525. That seems like a simple method for computing price; it is, if it were to stop there. But generally other charges are left unmentioned such as labor for chimney work, fireplace, window sills, door sills, fancy brick work, and so on.

To prevent all sorts of extras you need to insert a special term in the contract. Consider the following:

"The price is $_____ (includes all taxes except GST) based on a fixed sum for the work. Or, alternatively, the subcontractors' price is _____(includes all taxes except GST) based on the following formula [state formula]. Extra is added for the following: [list the items with respective prices]. Except as listed in the preceding, the subcontractor waives the right to charge further extras for work performed unless specifically agreed to in writing by the parties."

4. Providing for a holdback

Some people think a holdback represents money held to guarantee that work is performed properly. This may be so, but a holdback is provided to protect owner-builders against claims made by people under the subcontractor or material supplier (unpaid persons or companies supplying either labor or materials to the subcontractor or material supplier).

You, as owner-builder, want to avoid liability for those unpaid bills subcontractors or material suppliers have incurred for labor and materials as a result of the contract with you.

The holdback is generally determined by taking a percentage of the contract price. If progress advances are paid it represents a percentage of the advance. A percentage of funds is held back as trust money for a certain period of time for claims that might be made by persons or companies under the subcontractor or material supplier.

When you don't provide for a holdback and claims are made, you may have to pay a certain percentage of the contract over again, as specified under provincial law.

The percentage of holdback varies from province to province:

(a) In Manitoba the percentage holdback is 7.5%.

(b) In Newfoundland, Nova Scotia, Ontario, Saskatchewan, and British Columbia it is 10%.

(c) In Alberta it is 15%.

(d) In Prince Edward Island and New Brunswick it is 20% on contracts valued at $15 000 or less and 15% on contracts exceeding $15 000.

(e) In Quebec the amount of holdback is the sum owed to workers and suppliers by the subcontractor, who must supply owner-builders with a statement of debts when the bill is presented.

By withholding the specified percentage from the final payment or a progress advance for the time allowed by creditors under provincial law to register a lien against your property, you are protected.

Anyone making a claim under the subcontractor or material supplier has a specified number of days to provide you with notice, either by a registered letter to you or by registering a claim for lien against your property at the office of public records. So before you release holdback funds to a subcontractor or material supplier, you need to search the title of your property to see if liens are registered.

The time period allowed for registering a lien runs from 30 to 60 days after the work is substantially complete or abandoned:

(a) Newfoundland: 30 days

(b) British Columbia, Saskatchewan, and Manitoba: 40 days

(c) Nova Scotia, Ontario, and Alberta: 45 days

(d) New Brunswick and Prince Edward Island: 60 days

(e) Quebec: 30 days

Let's consider an example of a claim in Ontario. Claims under subcontractors or material suppliers must be made within 45 days of substantial completion. Suppose the electrician finishes the contract on April 30 and submits the final bill on that day for the sum of $5 000.

Rather than releasing the total $5 000, you hold back 10% as required by provincial law, or $500 for a period of 45 days. On June 15, you go down to the office of public records to check the title of your property to ascertain if the electrician's creditors have registered a lien against your property. If no liens are recorded or you haven't received a registered letter about a claim for lien you can safely release the $500 holdback to the electrician.

But, if you discover a lien registered against your property, you must forward a letter to the electrician stating that the funds are frozen because a lien is registered by one of their creditors and that they have to deal with your lawyer. You should then make a copy of the registered lien and of your contract with the electrician, and then deliver both documents to your lawyer.

In practice, you will rarely find liens against your property. But if you release all the funds to the electrician and don't hold back the $500 as prescribed by provincial law, a creditor of the electrician could require you to pay them $500 even though you paid off the electrician.

To protect yourself against claims made by creditors of subcontractors or material suppliers, consider adding a term similar to the following:

> "The subcontractor or material supplier acknowledges the right of the owner-builder to retain a holdback for construction or mechanic's liens as specified by provincial law."

5. Special permits

In addition to the main building permit required before work can begin, special permits are also needed at different stages of construction. They relate to electrical, plumbing, heating, landscaping, septic tank, and field beds, etc. As owner-builder you are ultimately responsible for all permits, but in practice, special permits are normally obtained by the subcontractor responsible for doing the specific work. The subcontractor knows when and where to call for inspections, so he or she should obtain the permits and arrange for inspections and approvals.

However, the quotations you receive from subcontractors may not mention this step, so you might want to add the following term:

> "The subcontractor is responsible for obtaining and paying for

special permits. This includes the responsibility of the subcontractor to request inspections and obtain approvals for the work covered by the permit before submitting an account for payment of an advance or the price."

6. When does the subcontractor commence work?

If the quotation states that the work shall commence within a certain number of days after signing, determine whether you can have the site ready. Quite frequently quotations are received months before actual construction starts. Delays are common, making it difficult to determine a starting date.

If you think time may be a problem, consider adding this term:

> "The subcontractor shall commence work within [state a period of time that represents the leeway subcontractors stated they needed before starting the work] of receiving notice from the owner-builder to commence work. If the subcontractor fails to commence the work in the time provided without receiving an extension, the owner-builder is at liberty to hire another subcontractor to perform the work. Time shall be of the essence."

7. Unforeseen changes?

After building begins, some changes are inevitable. A subcontractor may use this opportunity to make substantial profits by charging exorbitant extras for every conceivable change made after the contract is finalized. To cover this problem, consider adding the following term:

"No extra charges are payable for additional work due to changes made after the contract is finalized unless a price in writing is agreed to by both parties."

8. Workers' compensation laws

Provincial laws require subcontractors to have workers' compensation coverage for their employees. This insurance protects you in the case of employees being injured while working on your job site. Instead of suing you, they file a claim with the provincial agency. You should require that subcontractors show evidence of coverage and include the following clause in the quotation form:

"The subcontractor shall maintain workers' compensation coverage for all persons in their control working on the owner-builder's job site as required by provincial law and provide evidence of coverage in good standing."

9. Public liability and property damage

What happens if there is an injury to a member of the public on the job site? Private insurance coverage is available to protect against this potential liability. It is common to require subcontractors to provide an endorsement of their builder's risk insurance covering your job site. You could add the following clause:

"The subcontractor agrees to provide proof of builder's risk insurance in effect to the amount of at least $1 000 000 liability prior to commencing work, including general liability insurance and automobile liability insurance."

10. Guarantee for work and materials

Subcontractors may not mention guarantees, but if you think it is important, consider negotiating a guarantee as part of the contract. Here is a term you could insert:

"The subcontractor warrants all work and materials pursuant to this agreement for a period of ___ year(s) from completion. When the date of completion is in dispute, the date is presumed to correspond to the date when final payment became payable unless otherwise proved."

d. POTENTIAL PROBLEMS WHEN DEALING WITH MATERIAL SUPPLIERS

Different problems may arise when dealing with material suppliers. For example, it is not uncommon to receive damaged or defective goods from material suppliers. Sometimes a defect is not discovered until the materials are installed into the house.

You need to implement an inspection procedure for making sure materials are carefully checked for defects, damages, or shortages. Otherwise you won't be able to pinpoint where the problem originated.

Occasionally, suppliers deliver materials too early. When those materials lay around, they could get stolen or damaged. Make sure materials are delivered when you need them; if they are delivered early, ensure that they remain at the risk of the supplier.

Some material suppliers are wonderful to deal with; others are difficult. During negotiations, find out if they will accept the return of damaged or defective materials. If so, are they willing to return and pick them up for replacement?

Ask if they have service and repair personnel available to conduct repairs and to replace defective materials. If they don't, how are problems going to be remedied? Don't rely on a manufacturer's warranty.

Even though it is difficult, get the suppliers to address all your concerns. If you don't protect yourself, you may end up paying twice for the same materials. Suppliers and supplier-manufacturers will not hesitate in telling you that it's your problem. Some look after problems and others try to duck them.

If, after investigating suppliers, you still have concerns, follow up with a letter indicating that you accept their quotation provided they agree to your conditions. List your conditions in a letter using the method we identified in the preceding chapter. Later, if they deliver defective or damaged materials or send them prematurely, you have some protection. Consider using the clauses discussed below.

1. Provide specific times for delivery

Consider inserting the following clause to protect yourself from goods being delivered too early:

> "The material supplier agrees to deliver materials only after they are requested by the owner-builder or his or her designated agent. If delivery takes place before a request is made, then the goods remain at the risk of the supplier until they are incorporated into the structure. Without limiting the generality of this condition, the supplier is responsible for theft or damage that might ensue thereafter."

2. Provide for defects and damages and get a warranty

To address the potential problem of defective materials, use the following clause:

> "The material supplier shall return to pick up and replace materials set aside as defective, damaged, or unsatisfactory. The material supplier warrants the quality of materials that are installed and incorporated into the house for a period of [e.g., one year] from the date of installation."

Address the issue of warranty with this clause:

> "If defects are discovered during the warranty period, then the supplier shall return to repair or replace (which includes all labor and materials) the defective materials provided the request is in writing and made within the warranty period."

3. Negotiate favorable payment terms

Remember to negotiate favorable terms of payment. Suppliers extend terms to builders, and you can negotiate similar terms for yourself. Supply credit references and possibly your banker's name. When material suppliers are assured that you have adequate financing and good credit, they will be more comfortable to extend favorable terms.

The more time you have to pay the better. Time saves you interest charges, and if problems or discrepancies occur, you have a stronger bargaining position when money is owing.

12

PREPARE A BUILDING COST BUDGET

Even before you draw up your contracts, you need to prepare a budget, which is a reasonable estimate of the total building costs after assessing quotations and making preliminary cost estimates. This chapter explains what a building budget is and outlines the steps for preparing a detailed budget.

a. BUDGET FORECASTING

1. What is a budget?

A budget is your best estimate of the cost of materials and labor for your project. You need to forecast in advance each component cost so you have an idea of the estimated amount of money you expect to spend from the beginning to the end of the project.

Good forcasting enables you to compare actual costs of building at different stages of construction as the house goes up. Your budget should give you a good indication of what current costs are for building the project. It is important to prepare an accurate budget analysis.

2. What are the main reasons for preparing a budget?

A budget is important for a variety of reasons. It can gauge actual costs as they are coming in. You can compare actual costs against budget estimates by comparing running totals.

Use your budget to monitor costs. It will indicate when costs start getting out of hand. If costs reach somewhere between 4% and 5% over the budget forecast, take corrective measures such as cutting back on extras, holding off on purchasing built-in appliances, eliminating luxuries, and possibly re-tendering the remaining jobs.

A budget forecast can also give a good indication of value. Appraisers are less likely to fly in the face of your budget request if it is clear, detailed, and reasonably accurate.

Your budget supports the appraiser because he or she uses a less sophisticated approach for estimating value. Often a rounded square foot building cost formula is used similar to the method discussed in earlier chapters. But a detailed budget tends to be more accurate because the cost estimates are current and, therefore, more persuasive. It could actually assist the appraiser when he or she formulates their value approach by adjusting them to reflect current costs.

A budget forecast provides another aid; it implies that you have a good grasp on what is involved in terms of dollar value to build. Your builder capabilities are important. Lending officers assess applicant's building ability, especially when a loan based on a projected cost involves a large amount of money. A detailed budget can convince lenders that you've taken the time to learn and discover the costs involved in building a home.

b. PREPARING A DETAILED BUDGET

When preparing a budget, you should compare three quotations for every particular job. However, when budget forecasting, use the highest estimate unless that amount is outrageous compared the other two estimates. By using the highest estimate, you give yourself a buffer to cover unexpected increases in actual costs.

Inexperienced builders commonly forget to budget some items. Costly changes, unavoidable increases, and forgotten items often result in actual costs going over budget estimates. A well-prepared budget anticipates cost increases, so be sure to take a liberal approach when selecting estimates.

You don't want to risk having to re-apply for more financing later because you budgeted too low. During the building phase, it is much more difficult to arrange for additional financing, especially when under pressure from creditors. Avoid telling those you owe money to that you made an error. Creditors get nervous and sometimes register liens to protect their interest. Faced with liens you will incur more costs and even more difficulty arranging additional financing.

At the back of the book, Appendix 5 shows a format you can use for your budget forecasting. This is the document you present with your financing application. You can see by looking at Appendix 5 that the budget follows the general order of construction. In some cases, estimates are received through invited quotes (see Appendixes 3 and 4), and in other cases simply by calling for a verbal estimate. Fill in the blanks under the appropriate columns, add running totals, and you arrive at a total estimated building cost figure.

Using the left side of the form in Appendix 5, start at the first column, which is the cost classification. Next, to the right, is the estimated cost for that item, followed by a running total, then the actual cost, and a separate column for a running cost difference.

Let's begin filling in the budget columns, starting first with general items.

1. General items

(a) Drawings

The first classification covers the cost of drawings. This figure includes costs for plans and specifications including a plot plan. If the cost of the plot plan hasn't been included, contact an architectural draftsperson or preferably a surveyor. Obtain an estimate for the estimated cost of this plan. Enter all the costs together for drawings.

(b) Municipal charges

The next classification, municipal costs, includes the building department's charges for permit fees, lot levies, etc. Notice that permit fees, lot levies, and application fees are added together and entered under this classification.

(c) Survey fees

The survey fees involve more than just the normal survey. This classification calls for all surveying services. During construction the surveyor makes field trips to the job site. On the first trip, the surveyor stakes the lot. On the second trip, he or she designates the positioning of the foundation walls on the footings. The third trip is made just before final grading; the surveyor then instructs (according to the grading plan) the grading excavator where to cut, level, and slope the lot.

Later the surveyor makes a return trip to verify that the ground slopes properly. When satisfied, the surveyor files with the building department a grading certificate stating that the lot is graded in compliance with either the grading subdivision plan or good drainage practice.

Finally, the surveyor submits a building location plan and a survey report for your records and for the mortgage company.

When asking for an estimate of surveying costs, get a quote that covers all of the services. Enter a total cost estimate for all of the surveying services.

(d) Lawyer fees

The lawyer fees include both purchasing the lot and arranging mortgage financing. Mortgage financing involves legal fees to set up the mortgage and cover mortgage advances when funds are requested. At least three advances are normally made during construction for paying bills from subcontractors, material suppliers, and others.

Before mortgage advances are released, the lawyer checks the property title. Primarily he or she is looking for construction liens, although other potential charges are searched as well. Before releasing the advance, the lawyer makes sure no claims are made against the mortgage advance by creditors. The same procedure is conducted each time a release of funds is requested.

To estimate legal fees, ask for all the fees and disbursements involved in purchasing the building lot, setting up the mortgage, and releasing advances.

(e) Administration costs

Administration costs cover interest charges, realty taxes, fuel, hydro, and water charges. The longer the project takes, the higher the administrative costs. An estimate somewhere around 4% to 5% of the estimated total building cost should be enough.

(f) Insurance premiums

For insurance premiums, contact your insurance agent. Explain your building plans. Get an estimate for the cost of insurance to protect your site against theft, fire, wind storm, malicious damage, public liability, and property damage. Ensure that your agent convinces you the deductible limits make sense. Premium amounts differ depending on coverage and the deductible.

Simply paying a premium to say you have insurance makes no sense if the deductible amount is so high that your claim is wiped out because of a high deductible. Enter the estimated cost of insurance premiums.

(g) General labor

General labor refers to the miscellaneous areas of work where you can't pin the job to a specific subcontractor. It may include general clean up, pick and shovel, rough carpentry, and so forth. You and your family can minimize costs by doing these jobs yourselves.

If you do the work yourself, no estimate is needed here. Otherwise, estimate general labor costs at about 1¼% of the estimated project cost.

2. Well drilling

Fill this section in when the building lot has no municipal water services available.

Well drillers base costs on a flat amount or lineal foot basis depending on the depth.

Check with health authorities and ask about well records in your area. Find out the average depth of wells in the area. If estimates are unavailable from well drillers, provide your best estimate from your research.

3. Excavating

Under this section there are costs for stripping top soil, excavating the hole, trenching, and installing water and sewer lines. After the foundation is constructed there is back-filling and rough grading. There are also costs for grading to cut and slope, and costs for placing and leveling top soil and gravel.

If materials are not supplied, owner-builders will need an estimate for the cost of materials such as gravel, stone, and top soil.

4. Footings and foundation

Next you need an estimated cost for cribbing and forming the footings and an estimate for constructing the foundation. For this purpose you need to determine how the walls are constructed — by poured concrete, concrete block, or wood. Does the cost to construct include materials? If not, get an estimated cost for materials.

5. Dampproofing

The method of dampproofing foundation walls depends on the type of foundation material specified. The subcontractor that installs the foundation can tell you who to contact to get an estimated cost.

Some building codes have recently changed for dampproofing. There are now requirements for a moisture shield to wrap around the outside foundation walls after it's dampproofed. Both cost estimates have to be entered.

6. Weeping tile and gravel

Weeping tile and gravel work is usually installed by the same subcontractor that installs the footings. That subcontractor can assist you with your estimate. Make sure that the cost to supply and level gravel inside the foundation walls is included.

7. Framing materials

Get an estimated cost for the lumber to frame the house. This includes a materials list for lumber, nails, steel beams, steel posts, poly, and so forth. Lumberyards can provide itemized estimates.

8. Framing labor

The framer's labor costs include the cost of building the wood framing structure, which includes placing steel beams, building bearing walls in the basement, floor(s), walls, roofing structure (including assembling truss members if necessary), and installing windows and doors. After the basement floor is poured, there is also the cost for strapping the inside walls of the foundation.

9. Roofing

The roofers install the shingles and flashing on top of the framer's roof deck. They can provide an estimated labor cost. When materials are the responsibility of the owner-builder, then you need an estimated cost for roofing materials.

10. Concrete floor finishers

Contact concrete floor finishers for estimates for supplying, placing, and surface finishing the concrete basement floor and the garage floors. Generally they supply both concrete materials and labor.

11. Mechanical systems

Mechanical costs cover plumbing, heating, cooling, and electrical systems. If you plan to install optional systems such as security, intercom, or central vacuuming, you need individual costs for those items as well.

Contact mechanical subcontractors for estimates. Determine who is supplying materials. If materials are your responsibility, get an estimated cost for those materials.

12. Insulation and vapor barrier

Contact companies installing insulation and vapor barrier for estimates. If you have to supply the materials, get a price estimate.

13. Ceiling and wall covering board

With most new homes today, boarding consists of drywall rather than plaster. Contact either drywallers or plasterers for an estimate to cover ceilings and walls. If materials are your responsibility, contact boarding subcontractors and ask them to provide a materials list with their labor estimate.

14. Exterior wall covering

The cost for the exterior walls depends on the type of materials specified. Are the walls covered with brick, cladding, or some other product? With masonry products like brick, you have to contact a masonry supplier for the cost to supply materials. Bricklayers only provide the labor estimate.

When using conventional siding such as aluminum or vinyl, contact siding subcontractors for estimates. If you supply the materials, obtain a materials list to get a cost.

With so-called "maintenance-free" homes, the siding installer covers wood trim areas that otherwise would need periodic painting such as soffit, fascia, and framing areas. Contact material suppliers. They can measure and list the materials for obtaining an estimated cost.

15. Eavestrough and downspouts

Ask for a cost to supply and install eavestrough and downspouts. Materials are mostly made from aluminum, galvanized metal, or copper depending on what is specified.

16. Roof flashing and caulking

Be sure to get your roofer to go back and re-examine roof areas after exterior walls and chimneys are finished. Add a miscellaneous amount for the roofer's time and services to finish items if necessary. Generally an estimate of approximately a half of a percent of the estimated building cost is sufficient.

17. Septic tank and field bed

For building lots that don't have municipal sewage available, contact experienced and licensed private sewage disposal subcontractors for an estimate to install the septic tank, distribution box, and field bed. Their cost estimate generally covers all materials.

18. Ceiling insulation

In cases where ceiling insulation is blown, you need a separate cost for supplying and installing the insulation. Contact the same subcontractor who installed insulation and vapor barrier for an estimated cost.

19. Ceramic tile and bathroom accessories

The ceramic tile suppliers generally have their own installers for ceramic tubs, shower stalls, and floors. Ask them to include the cost for the bathroom accessories such as the soap dishes, paper tile holders, and towel racks. Cost estimates are obtained from carpet and tile stores.

20. Floor coverings

Floor coverings include resilient flooring, ceramic tile, hardwood floors, and carpeting, depending on what is specified. Most carpet and tile stores supply all floor coverings. For hardwood, a separate supplier and installer may be needed. Itemize each flooring type separately; obtain cost estimates for each type of floor covering specified.

21. Kitchen cupboards and vanities

Manufacturers of kitchen cupboards and vanities usually employ installers. Estimates for cupboards, vanities, and countertops normally include supplying and installing. When they don't, try the trimming carpenter.

22. Built-in appliances

The water heater is either purchased or rented. In either case, it must be connected by a plumber and perhaps an electrician. Factor in the estimated cost for supplying and connecting all built-in appliances such as the water heater, dishwasher, garburator, and stove.

23. Hardware, trim, shelving, and mirror supplier

Contact either a lumberyard or a trim supplier for an estimated cost for the hardware, trim, shelving, and mirrors. Either one will measure and itemize a cost estimate.

24. Trimming carpenter

The trim carpenter installs all finished trim, hardware, shelving, and mirrors.

Trim carpenters can provide an estimated cost to trim out the house.

25. Painting and decorating

Painters provide cost estimates to paint inside and outside. Determine who supplies the materials. If it is your responsibility, get a list and an estimated cost.

26. Electrical fixtures

The electrical fixtures are normally supplied by the owner-builder rather than the electrician. Building products suppliers and electrical fixture supply stores have all kinds of fixtures for lighting the rooms from the chandelier in the dining room to lighting in the bedrooms.

27. Landscaping

The landscaping ranges from the walkway and driveway coverings to decking, fencing, sodding, or seeding. Obtain cost estimates for each of those items.

The sections above cover the individual items to cost out detailed items for covering labor and material supplies to build your new home. All estimates are added together as running totals under the heading in the second column. After adding the estimated costs and the extras, you can arrive at an estimated building cost total.

As you can see, a budget is an important measuring stick. It takes considerable time to complete all the detailed estimates, but it will help you determine how much money you need to finance the project. By monitoring actual costs against the budget forecast, you can see if corrective measures are needed to keep within the total budget target.

13

FINANCING NEW HOME CONSTRUCTION

Financing is needed during the building stages in order to get the project off the ground. Without adequate financing, projects are doomed from the start. While your existing financial resources and income earning ability are important, you still have to be careful to apply for the right type of financing.

Choose a financing package that ensures you will have enough money. At the same time, arrange for a take-out mortgage covering a term and an amortization matching your present and future financial obligations. You want to plan for your future financial freedom. Keep in mind your other financial responsibilities and choose the best financing plan for your lifestyle.

a. THE TWO STAGES OF FINANCING

Few building projects ever get off the ground without financing. You should be aware of the potential problems in trying to finance a house that does not exist.

Good financing proposals sometimes get turned down because the wrong lending institution was approached. Sometimes lending officers lack sufficient knowledge about particular financing options for new home construction. Sometimes financing requests are misdirected in the first place. But first you should realize that there are two stages of financing: financing to cover the property for a term of years after the house is complete (a mortgage) and funding to pay the bills during the constructing stage.

b. ABOUT MORTGAGES

A mortgage is a loan. Borrowers put up real property as security for the loan. As an owner-builder, the only property you have available as security is likely your building lot. But the value of vacant land without a house is insufficient as security to support a mortgage loan for building purposes except in rare situations.

If your building lot is worth $50 000, and the total project including land is worth $150 000 based on your budget forecast, you need $100 000 financing. But $50 000 worth of land security is insufficient value to support a $100 000 project loan.

1. The conventional mortgage

The most common type of take-out mortgage is a conventional mortgage. Major lenders offer conventional mortgages because they represent the largest profit portfolio with the best security. Conventional lenders, however, are restricted by law and cannot lend more than 75% of the property value except under special circumstances. Therefore the loan to value ratio (the percentage) for a conventional mortgage can never exceed 75% of property value.

Value for mortgage purposes is always defined as the lesser of either the selling price for the property or its appraised value. Using the previous illustration of $150 000, if the appraiser assesses value at $140 000 instead of the $150 000 agreed to between the parties, then property value for maximum mortgage lending purposes is based on $140 000. Lenders take 75% of the lower amount (value) for determining the maximum loan amount instead of the purchase price.

If the appraiser accepts the purchase price, then for a conventional mortgage the borrower can obtain a maximum mortgage loan of $112 500 (75% of $150 000). The borrower has to contribute the remaining $37 500; the down payment represents the borrower's investment or equity in the property.

If you need a loan that is more than 75% of the property value, you must apply for a high-ratio mortgage loan instead of the conventional mortgage.

2. The insured mortgage

To obtain a loan greater than 75% of property value, your only alternative is to apply for a high-ratio mortgage. Major lenders, however, cannot issue high-ratio mortgages unless they are insured. With insured mortgages, you can apply for loans of up to 90% of property value.

There are, of course, special situations where lending amounts can go as high as 95% of the property value. As an owner-builder, you should keep in mind the insured mortgage. Even where you may plan on investing more than 25% of your own money into the project, an insured mortgage has advantages over a conventional mortgage for building purposes.

For example, let's say the property has a value of $150 000. Under an insured mortgage you can apply for a maximum loan amount of $135 000 which is $22 500 greater than the maximum loan for a conventional mortgage. It reduces the borrower's contribution or down payment in the project: compared to a conventional mortgage, it drops from $37 500 to $15 000.

Canada Mortgage and Housing Corporation (CMHC) and G.E. Capital Mortgage Company offer insured mortgages. Right now, G.E. Capital Mortgage Company does not have policy guidelines set for new construction loans.

CMHC sets guidelines for conventional lenders who are listed as approved to administer insured mortgage loans. You can apply for lending amounts up to 90% of the property value instead of being limited to borrowing only 75% under a conventional mortgage.

Another important distinction to keep in mind about insured mortgages is that they are offered to owner-builders looking to finance during the house construction. So if you've invested money into land and you want to finance the building part, then you can apply for an insured mortgage as an interim financing option. Even when borrowers intend to invest more than 25% of their savings into the project, which complies with the 75% rule for a conventional mortgage, an insured mortgage still proves more advantageous for owner builders.

Some lending officers are unfamiliar with the CMHC guidelines, especially those related to new construction, so it is no wonder that it is difficult to secure financing. Be sure to seek out lenders who are issuing the insured type of mortgage.

For information about insured mortgages, contact your local office of CMHC. Ask a representative for names of approved lenders, those who are active and take a sympathetic view to help owner builders with their financial needs.

Lenders approved to issue CMHC insured mortgages are chartered banks, trust companies, life insurance companies, loan companies and credit unions — practically all major lending institutions. But again, not all of them are receptive to insured mortgages for building projects.

Lenders who issue insured mortgages enjoy certain advantages. If a borrower defaults or fails to make payments, the lenders have a guarantee that enables them to call on CMHC to bail them out by requesting that the loan balance be paid off. The borrower still loses his or her equity. For the privilege of obtaining an insured mortgage, CMHC charges a fee for guaranteeing the loan to its approved lenders. This is an added cost in comparison to a conventional mortgage.

The additional premium, however, is more than justified and reasonable if you need a high-ratio mortgage or if you can't secure interim financing during the building stages. The premium outweighs having to apply for a high-ratio mortgage elsewhere.

3. The high-risk or equity mortgage

The third type of mortgage is a high-risk or equity mortgage. Private individuals and junior lending companies issue this type of mortgage when other lenders won't. They are referred to as "lenders of last resort."

High-risk lenders don't restrict themselves to value ratios like the 75% rule for conventional mortgages or the 90% rule for insured mortgages. Also, they are not restricted by policy rules concerning the borrower's source of income.

With this kind of mortgage, expect high interest rates, bonus charges, and brokerage fees as additional costs. These added fees, charges, and costs for borrowing means interest rates that are sometimes double or triple those for a conventional or insured mortgage; they represent a major obstacle against applying for this type of loan.

Published mortgage rates in most daily newspapers have no application to high-risk or equity lenders. You can find high-risk and equity lenders by contacting mortgage brokers, lawyers, and personal loan companies.

c. INTERIM FINANCING OPTIONS

How do you finance during the construction stages? Obviously, after the project is built it's relatively easy to finance; you simply apply for one of the three types of mortgages discussed above. But your building project is not complete, and you need money to pay for materials, subcontractor accounts, and other costs. That is why you should delay deciding on the type of mortgage until you decide on the best interim financing option for your circumstances. The best interim financing often dictates the type of mortgage you select.

The most popular types of interim financing options are bridge loans, operating lines of credit, and progress draw interim mortgages. Each one of them has its advantages and disadvantages.

1. The bridge loan

As the name suggests, a bridge loan provides money to bridge the time from the start of construction to when a take-out mortgage is obtained after the house is complete. The bridge loan is money given to borrowers from the start of construction. The amount borrowed is set aside and available for paying building debts during the course of construction. Interest on bridge loans is charged against the full amount that accrues each day until it's paid off.

Bridge loans are hard to obtain because lenders frown on lending large amounts without having liquid security equal to the amount they lend. Lenders prefer security easily convertible to cash. With this type of security, lenders are willing to set up bridge loans to provide interim financing for the construction stages only.

Unfortunately, most borrowers don't have this type of security available to offer. Also, paying interest on the total loan approved from the start is an expensive method of financing a building project; paying interest on money sitting idle until the invoices come in from building accounts is not a cost effective borrowing option.

2. The operating line of credit

The second type of interim financing is a revolving credit limit pre-arranged with a lender known as an operating line of credit. Lenders approve a maximum loan amount, but instead of setting aside funds as with a bridge loan, they reserve a maximum amount to be drawn against by the borrower. So when you need money, funds are drawn against the credit limit arranged and interest is charged only against the amount drawn. Cheques are written at the borrowers' discretion to pay bills and accounts up to the loan contract amount.

An operating line, like a bridge loan, is also difficult to arrange without liquid assets as security. If you have access to savings bonds, stocks, or other securities, then an operating line of credit is an excellent financing option because you pay interest only on the amount you draw down.

3. Progress draw-interim mortgage

A progress draw-interim mortgage is a mortgage for the total amount of financing based on the estimated value of the project as if the house were built. Value is determined by the lower amount of either the appraised value of the property as a completed project or the amount you've assigned in your application form using your estimated budget forecast.

During specific stages of construction, advances are requested against the approved mortgage loan. An inspection is conducted, and for each advance the project must have value added to justify releasing an advance of money.

A lawyer searches the property title to determine if liens or other charges are registered against the property. If the property is clear, funds are advanced based on the work completed to date. As in the operating line of credit, interest is charged on the funds advanced.

Today, no more than a handful of lenders offer progress draw-interim mortgages. The best source for this type of financing arrangement is CMHC; they offer this as an interim financing option and they encourage owner-builders to apply for them.

There are several good reasons why owner-builders should seriously consider applying for a CMHC-insured mortgage as an interim financing option:

(a) Interest is charged only on the amount of money drawn, not on the total loan approved.

(b) A progress draw-interim mortgage serves two functions: funding for financing the construction, and after the building project is complete, financing for a term of years. The mortgage automatically converts or flips to a take-out mortgage, eliminating additional legal fees, appraisal fees, and other mortgage costs for setting up a take-out mortgage.

(c) CMHC has fewer restrictions against geographical areas compared to lenders issuing conventional loans. With conventional loans, some lenders are reluctant to approve mortgages in certain areas, especially in rural settings where no municipal services are available and where property sales are slower.

(d) As a builder, your capabilities are not scrutinized as they are when you apply for a mortgage that isn't backed by a CMHC guarantee.

(e) You only draw the amount you need. If you need less financing than the mortgage amount arranged, the loan amount is automatically adjusted down without incurring additional penalty.

(f) CMHC interim mortgage loans converted to closed take-out mortgages with terms greater than three years are automatically eligible for payouts after three years, based on a maximum three months' interest

penalty, a privilege rarely available with other closed mortgages.

CMHC mortgage financing is attractive as an interim financing option, especially for owner-builders. It's probably the only practical financing method for high-ratio mortgage situations and for interim financing while the house is in the constructing stages.

However, a CMHC progress draw mortgage has additional charges for the insurance premium and inspection fees on advances. But those costs are minimized when you consider the added administrative costs to set up two loans: one for interim financing using a bridge loan or operating line of credit, and another for a take-out mortgage when the house construction is complete. Unlike CMHC interim progress draw mortgages, the other interim financing packages are not automatically flipped over to a take-out mortgage without incurring additional costs.

d. CMHC PROGRESS DRAW GUIDELINES

There are many ways that a CMHC mortgages can work to your advantage. Loans offered to owner-builders are available for building single family homes and for semi-detached, duplex, and triplex homes as well.

The CMHC-insured mortgage loan to value ratio, as previously mentioned, goes to as high as 90% of the appraised value. But limits are set depending on the repayment option selected between an equal payment mortgage (EPM) or a variable rate mortgage (VRM).

With equal payment mortgages (EPM) the maximum loan amount is 90% of the first $180 000 of the lending value plus 80% of the remainder. With a variable rate mortgage

(VRM) the maximum loan amount is 85% of the first $180 000 plus 80% of the remainder.

For example, suppose you selected an equal payment mortgage and your lending value is $225 000. CMHC will approve a maximum loan of:

90% of the first $180 000 equals	$162 000
80% of remainder ($45 000) equals	36 000
maximum EPM loan amount	$198 000

In the case of variable rate mortgages the maximum loan amount is calculated as follows:

85% of the first $180 000 equals	$153 000
80% of the remainder ($45 000) equals	36 000
maximum VRM loan amount	$189 000

The maximum amortization period is 40 years for an equal payment mortgage and 25 years for a variable rate mortgage.

Amortization shouldn't be confused with the term of mortgage. Amortization simply means the length of time it takes to pay off the loan if the same payments are made during monthly intervals at a fixed rate of interest. The term of mortgage is strictly related to time and has nothing to do with whether the mortgage amount gets paid in full.

Borrowing for homes involves larger amounts of money compared to chattels like furniture and cars. To keep monthly payments reasonable, usually loan balances are outstanding at the end of mort-gage terms that are normally arranged for mortgages. Therefore, the total payments made during the term of mortgage rarely are large enough to pay off the loan when the term expires. Instead the balance is re-written for another term until the loan eventually gets paid in full.

Mortgage terms are usually negotiated for periods from six months to five years, though it is possible to arrange longer terms. However the majority of mortgages are negotiated for shorter terms for the convenience of re-negotiating the interest. The minimum mortgage term set by CMHC for insured mortgages is six months.

Applicants for a CMHC mortgage loan must own their building lot, but the lot does not have to be paid for in full.

These guidelines are designed for owner-builders. The intent is to prevent builders' direct involvement. It is specified that each contract an owner-builder enters into cannot exceed 50% of the building costs for the unit. This prevents builders from circumventing the special rules owner-builders enjoy, especially when they don't have to enroll in provincial warranty programs like builders.

Construction cannot start until CMHC gives approval to the plans and specifications. Once approved the plans and specifications are required to be posted on the site.

During the building stages, CMHC carries out inspections, normally during three stages of construction. First, when the foundation is complete and everything is ready for backfilling; a second inspection when the roof is installed, all rough-ins complete, and the house ready for interior boarding; and a third and final inspection when all work is complete.

Inspections ensure that the accepted plans and specifications are being followed, that the building work reasonably conforms to the National Building Code for new residential construction (similar to most provincial building codes), and that technical builders' bulletins are followed.

Rules are flexible for disbursing money and progress advances are worked out between owner-builders and the approved lender based on cash flow requirements and other considerations. A request for a progress advance can be made by telephone, personal visit, or by mailing a request form to the district office of CMHC.

Before authorizing a progress advance, CMHC ensures that sufficient funds are kept at all times to complete construction of the housing project. When a request for a progress advance is made, the project is inspected to determine the percentage stage of completion. The amount of advance depends on how much the project is worth based on a guide of percentages for specified work in place.

Materials delivered are not counted unless they are incorporated into the building. The amount of completion is compared to a breakdown of the different stages of construction converted to percentages. The guide to percentage completion is set out in Appendix 6. Note that each item is listed with appropriate percentages assigned for that particular item.

14

BUILDING PERMITS

As a general rule, owner-builders are not permitted to start any sort of construction without first obtaining a building permit. The chief building official in the municipality in which the building lot is located examines applications for permits.

a. OBTAIN PROVINCIAL CLEARANCE

In many cases, a provincial clearance may be necessary before making an application, filing building documents, and paying the fees to secure a building permit.

The bureaucracy is different depending on the circumstances of each case. Some applications are relatively straightforward while others involve time and confusion. Examine the flow chart in Figure #36. Note the intervening clearances that might be necessary before it is possible to go to the chief building permit.

To determine the necessary requirements in your case, examine the classification of your building lot. Does it have municipal services available? Does the lot fall within a classification of a recent plan of subdivision, a rural lot, or an infill lot in an urban area? (Refer back to chapter 2 for a discussion of these terms.)

The path to the chief building official is relatively easy when your lot is fully serviced and within a recent plan of subdivision.

But if the lot is unserviced and is classified as a rural or infill, then it gets more complicated. You could run into all sorts of preliminary approvals that might be required.

For example, if your lot falls within a flood plain, a defined fill area, or is near a provincial highway, then clearances are likely needed. When other agencies are directly involved, you can't go to your chief building official for a building permit until the clearances are obtained.

Remember, you have to contact the department of health or some provincial environmental agency to determine the requirements for obtaining clearances when they are necessary.

Every province has different procedures, but you can still get a sense from the flow chart in Figure #36 of what you might expect to run into, depending on the classification and location of the building lot.

b. PRESENT THE BUILDING DOCUMENTS

After obtaining the provincial clearances, you can apply directly before the chief building official for a building permit. Subject to some minor variations from area to area, you must submit a completed application form and two copies of the building documents, sufficiently detailed and illustrated according to a convenient scale, for examination which contain the following particulars:

(a) the foundation plan,

(b) the floor plans,

(c) exterior elevations,

(d) a cross section or cutaway view showing details of the size of component members and the proposed method for joining them together to form a complete structure,

(e) a plot or site plan showing the positioning of the building foundation on the building lot with distances from the front, side, and rear yards, the foundation and driveway measurements,

(f) a heat loss calculation and duct design showing details of the heating system and details of the cooling system if air conditioning is planned,

(g) a roof truss plan if roof trusses are proposed as a means for holding up the roof sheathing and shingles, instead of rafters and ceiling joists, and

(h) a grading plan prepared by a surveyor or engineer showing elevations designed to slope or grade the lot in such a way as to properly drain surface water away from the building, in an orderly fashion, according to a registered grading plan or good drainage practice.

When the building department examines the building documents, the chief building official determines if the proposed structure complies with building code provisions, zoning by-laws, drainage regulations, and other requirements for the area where the house is proposed to be constructed.

c. BUILDING CODE REGULATIONS

The building code is a collection of building practices and suggested specifications originally designed for providing minimum standards to protect the health, safety, and welfare of its occupants. But recent changes in some provinces suggest a broadening of the original mandate.

Those changes suggest other purposes such as requiring builders to maximize efficiency and economy of heating and cooling systems. Others require builders to maximize comfort and quality in living and basement areas by attempting to eliminate altogether environmental nuisance caused by noise, air quality, and moisture.

We don't know yet if these recent changes are succeeding or whether they are simply an intrusion that contributes unnecessarily to building costs — thus pushing affordable housing further out of the reach of the would-be new home buyer.

If your plans and specifications don't comply with building code provisions, or if the chief building official finds inconsistencies or contrary building practices illustrated by the building documents, the chief building official can either note changes that must be complied with or reject the plans and specifications altogether. Once rejected, a building permit cannot be issued until new or amended plans and specifications are re-submitted.

d. ZONING REGULATIONS

After passing building code requirements, the building documents are examined in light of existing zoning regulations. Zoning by-laws establish and regulate the use of land. They enable the municipality to co-ordinate land uses, protect areas by preventing incompatible uses, and establish appropriate standards for development.

There are two primary aspects of zoning to keep in mind. First, zoning provisions prohibit certain uses in geographical areas. Maps illustrate locations of geographical zones designating where certain uses are permitted. For example, if you want to build a two- or three-family home as opposed to a single-family home, you can refer to the maps to determine if the area where your lot is located permits that use of the land.

Second, zoning provisions regulate building setbacks, side and rear yard requirements, maximum lot coverage, and building heights. The chief building official examines your building documents to determine if the proposed project complies with those requirements.

If the chief building official discovers that your project doesn't comply with one or more zoning provisions, you could amend your documents, request a minor variance, or request a zoning amendment.

Ask for a variation from zoning regulations that are offended if the variation is minor in nature. For example, say you want to build three feet from a side yard in order to situate the house substantially inside the building area. If the by-law calls for a minimum of four feet, and the project in other respects complies with the rest of the zoning provisions, then you could ask for relief by making an application for a minor variance.

A tribunal is set up to hear your application, and if neighbors don't strongly object, then you could get a variance.

If the relief is deemed to be substantial, then you're better off requesting an amendment rather than a variance. When amendments are requested, the procedure is more complicated. Zoning amendments must comply with official plan provisions or policy statements established by local council related to development in your area before they are considered.

Contact your lawyer for advice on how to proceed with an application to amend zoning.

e. PERMIT FEES, LOT LEVIES, AND DEVELOPMENT CHARGES

When the chief building official is satisfied that building code, zoning, and other regulations are complied with, permit fees, lot levies, and development charges are calculated and payable. After payment, a building permit is issued on condition that at defined stages of construction, the chief building official performs on-site inspections to verify that the actual constructing procedures are in accordance with the building documents (plans and specifications approved or red lined) filed with the building department.

After the building permit is issued, you can go ahead with your building project by putting together a construction timetable to co-ordinate sub-trades and material suppliers.

FIGURE #36
FLOW CHART — MUNICIPAL ADVISORY

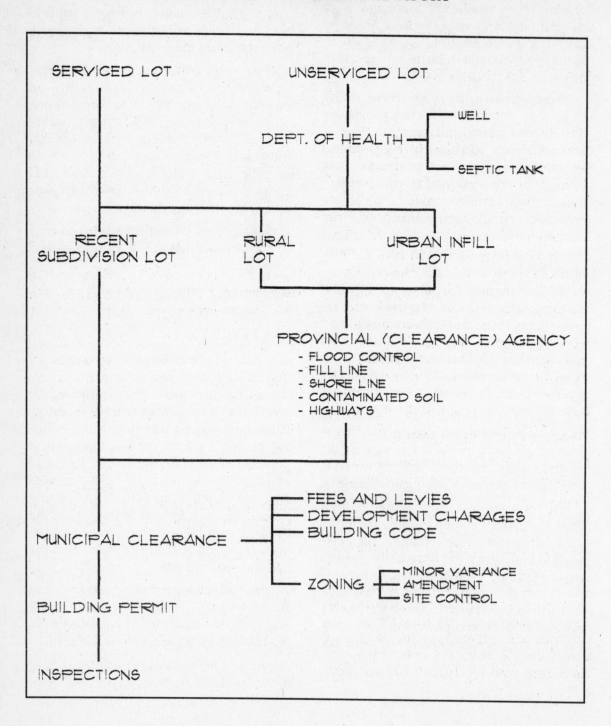

15

BASIC STRUCTURE AND SERVICES: PHASE ONE

This chapter and the following four chapters covers the steps involved for constructing your home. Construction is divided into five phases and an approximate time frame is provided for each phase to give you a guide for preparing your own timetable.

In total, all phases should take a maximum of four to six months. However, you must co-ordinate all the players in a timely manner. Appendix 7 at the back of this book shows a sample construction timetable. Appendixes 8 through 12 show flow charts for the five individual phases. Use those documents to see when each player gets involved; then you can co-ordinate them by devising your own timetable.

a. FOLLOW A SEQUENCE

Do not attempt to rush to completion by doubling up jobs, except where the flow charts note when certain jobs can safely proceed side by side. When sub-trades work out of sequence, it costs you money and it is potentially disruptive to the flow of the complete job.

For example, suppose you arrange for the electrician to install rough wiring before the plumbing and heating subcontractors are finished. If the wiring is directly in the path of plumbing pipes or duct runs, the electrician has to come back and re-route part of the wiring. In an attempt to rush, you've actually slowed progress. You also may incur extra charges for the time and materials to re-route the wiring.

b. PREPARE YOUR CONSTRUCTION TIMETABLE

The time identified at the beginning of each phase is, of course, an approximation. It can be lengthened or shortened depending on the time of year and your deadline. Refer to Appendix 7 and set your timetable in a similar manner, setting the times to match your deadlines. If your deadline is more urgent, adjust certain times to conform to the remaining time left for building.

Timetables must have some flexibility worked into them to allow for unknown contingencies such as inclement weather, sickness, and delays. Whenever timetables are revised, notify the rest of the sub-trades and material suppliers so they can re-arrange their schedules. Keep them informed. They don't work solely for you and can't afford to sit idle.

c. HOW TO PROCEED THROUGH THE FIVE PHASES

Carefully examine Appendixes 8 to 12. Relate those flow charts to Appendix 7, the main construction timetable, when you devise your own plan. When phase one is finished, begin the second and third phases almost simultaneously.

During phase two and three, you can double up because the second phase deals with interior work while the third deals with exterior work. However, when starting the third phase, make sure your electrician has installed the rough-in wiring for the outside. Otherwise, you could add more time and expense cutting away openings in exterior walls to complete the electrical system.

After completing phases two and three, proceed immediately to phase four and complete that stage before starting phase five. Although it is possible to double up in some instances between phases four and five, follow the sequence unless time is running out.

d. PHASE ONE — CONSTRUCTION DETAILING

Phase one, the construction detailing, has an estimated time frame of about four weeks. Contact all sub-trades and material suppliers involved in this phase at least a few weeks before they're actually needed. Co-ordinate a time schedule for this phase. Use the estimated times subcontractors stated they needed in their quotations. Make copies of your time schedule and circulate a copy to each sub-trade and material supplier.

1. Well driller

The well driller is first if the lot is unserviced. They dig or drill the well. When necessary, get together with the well driller and bring a copy of your plot plan. The terms should have been negotiated (see

chapters 10 and 11). Then co-ordinate the construction works.

2. Surveyor

The surveyor visits the job site, preferably after the excavator scrapes the top soil. The surveyor hammers into the ground several stakes instructing the excavator where and how deep to dig the excavation for footings and foundation walls.

The surveyor tells the excavator where to locate the excavated hole, how large of a perimeter to dig, and how deep to excavate the site. After footings are installed on the ground, the surveyor returns and marks the location for the foundation walls by designating where the outside corners of the foundation sits on the footings. This avoids any possibility of making a costly mistake of erecting foundation walls too close to property line clearances.

3. Excavator

The excavator arrives with machines. First the existing top soil is scraped off the surface of the ground, then it is mound in a convenient place, away from the proposed excavation site.

In a serviced lot, the excavator installs water and sewer lines by trenching from the property line directly into the excavated site where the inside walls of the proposed foundation will eventually be constructed. This enables the plumber to make connections to tie in water and sewer lines to the building.

Extra soil from the excavation is ramped beside the open cavity for concrete trucks to get high enough to pour the footings.

4. Building inspector-soil inspection

After the excavation, the soil is inspected to ensure it has adequate bearing qualities for

for the weight of footings, foundation, and house structure on the opened surface ground area.

If the soil is unsatisfactory, the building inspector orders corrective measures (or perhaps a soils report) to ensure that the construction will be placed on stable soil to prevent future damage by sinking, sagging, or settling.

5. Concrete footing former

When soils are satisfactory, the concrete former cribs the footings and forms the base for placing footings. Concrete is poured into the cribbing which hardens and forms. When the concrete is hard enough, the surveyor returns to pin the location for the foundation walls.

6. Foundation installer

The foundation installer could be one of three different subcontractors depending on your specifications.

If the walls are supposed to be poured concrete, then you use the same concrete formers who installed the footings. If the foundation is constructed of concrete block walls, then you hire a block layer to lay the block foundation. Once the block wall is laid, it has put over it a skim coating of concrete parging covering the exterior face to create a flat surface for dampproofing.

If the plans and specifications call for a preserved wood foundation, then a framer is hired to construct foundation walls of preserved wood.

7. Dampproof installer

After foundation walls are constructed, the outside surface area is dampproofed with a material to resist moisture. It is now recommended that a new, approved material be used for wrapping around the dampproofed areas of the foundation walls. The material might be drain clad or a paroc drainage media or any approved material placed between the dampproofed foundation wall and the backfill material to allow surface water to freely flow down the outside foundation wall to reach the weeping tile without causing water pockets that lay against the foundation and eventually leak into the interior basement. Under some building codes, the use of this new, approved material is now a requirement.

8. Weeping tile and gravel installer

The weeping tile and gravel installer places tile around the outside perimeter of the footings. The tile has perforated holes to allow water to enter and lead along the tile where water is directed into either a storm drain or more likely into a retaining reservoir below the basement floor. When water in the reservoir reaches a certain level, it's discharged by a sump pump onto the upper surface ground area or into a storm drain so that it is directed away from the foundation walls.

After the tile is installed, gravel is placed on top to protect it from being crushed under the weight of the backfill material. Gravel also acts as a filtering bed to obstruct ground material from seeping into the tile, building up, and plugging it.

This method doesn't work with some types of sand material, so the tile either has a sock placed around it or a felt blanket material is laid over the gravel. This prevents fine sand particles from running along with water into the tile which over time plugs it, preventing proper drainage.

The weeping tile and gravel installers also place gravel on the inside foundation walls over the excavated ground area so that when it's spread and raked, it levels flush with the top of the footings. However, this work is usually performed before the foundation walls are constructed shortly after the footings.

9. Permission to backfill

The building inspector is called to make an inspection of the site for permission to backfill. The inspector checks to make sure dampproofing (shielding material), the weeping tile, and the gravel are all properly installed before permission is granted to cover in.

10. Framing wood structure

The majority of new homes constructed today are built of wood. Basically the method used is platform framing. The old method of framing was known as balloon framing; the wall studs were erected before the floor systems and extended continuously from the foundation up to the roof line.

But with today's platform construction, the floor is built first on top of the foundation walls, using a wood floor joist and sub-floor system. Over the floor system, wall studs for one storey are erected. If the house has two stories then the second floor platform is assembled on top of the first storey stud walls, and a second set of stud walls one storey high is erected on top of the second floor assembly platform. This method is repeated to build a third storey and so forth.

Depending on your plans and specifications, the roof assembly is either stick built as with the rest of the framing, or roofing members are built off site by a truss manufacturer. Either method is acceptable and both perform similar functions, which is to hold up the roof sheathing and shingles.

However, with roof trusses, the roof load is easily transferred to the outside walls, which eliminates the necessity for interior bearing walls. This provides more flexibility for making changes by moving interior walls.

Also, as part of the framing job, windows and doors are installed by the framer. That means you need to co-ordinate delivery of windows and doors to avoid having them lay around where they can be easily damaged or stolen.

Later, after the basement floor is poured, the framer returns to strap basement walls with framing studs to accommodate the basement insulation. This takes place over the inside walls.

11. Framing inspection

Before proceeding with further inside work, a framing inspection approval is required. The building inspector conducts a routine check of the framing structure to ensure that good construction methods were employed according to the practices provided by the building code.

Accompany the building inspector when he or she conducts the inspection. Check to see if the framer installed backing material on framing members to allow boarding material to have backing to secure wall board to the stud walls. The building inspector will explain backing procedures and show you which areas to check. If proper backing is missed, call the framer back to complete the framing.

12. Septic system installer

If the building lot doesn't have municipal sewage service available, then a disposal system is installed on the property. The septic tank installer will install the sewage system after the health authorities inspect the soil and surrounding area.

13. Secure the premises

After the building inspector approves the framing, secure the structure and premises. Contact your finish carpenter to install locks on all doors and seal open areas to prevent unauthorized entry. Place "no trespassing signs" both at the driveway entrance and at the front of the outside framing structure.

This completes phase one. In the next chapter, we discuss phase two, which deals mostly with the interior work.

16

INTERIOR ROUGH-INS: PHASE TWO

a. PHASE TWO — CONSTRUCTION DETAILING

Phase two primarily deals with interior house construction, the rough-ins which are lines for services leading through the house that are generally covered over by concrete floors or interior boarding materials.

Using Appendix 7, prepare your timetable after personally discussing this phase of the work with the subcontractors involved (they are listed in Appendix 9). Coordinate dates for starting and finishing those jobs.

Follow and complete the steps in the order shown in Appendix 7. After the basement floor is finished and the walls and ceilings are closed-in, it is very expensive to make changes or corrections if you discover a mistake or find you have forgotten something. Carefully check to see that each step is properly finished. Verify its completion by conducting your own physical inspection of the premises.

b. THE STEPS

1. Plumber

The plumber comes first. Plumbers install underground plumbing in the basement by laying waste and vent pipes. After the base work is complete, the house is roughed-in by installing waste and venting pipes, as well as hot and cold water lines through the framing walls and ceilings.

For the water and effluent to freely drain, the waste system needs adequate venting. Venting performs three functions. First, it allows air in front of rushing water to escape. Second, it allows air to be reintroduced into the waste pipes after water passes. Last, it allows sewer gases to escape outside through the vent stack. Figure #37 illustrates a house venting system.

Later, your plumber returns to finish water lines and connect the water heater, waste piping, and venting in the basement. Then all the fixtures in the kitchen, bathrooms, and laundry area are installed after cupboards and vanities are affixed.

Remember, if you're finishing an area not identified for completion on the plans, you have to advise the plumber so he or she can finish roughing-in that area before walls and ceilings are covered over. Often problems occur when owner-builders decide to finish a room or area that wasn't originally planned for finishing.

For that matter, exercise caution by notifying all sub-trades that you decided in mid-stream to make changes or finish additional areas. Contact sub-trades listed in the flow chart in Appendix 9 for this phase of the work. Determine if they need to lay wires, pipe, or duct lines in the area you want finished. Otherwise, you may have to tear down boarding to allow access for those services, especially if they have to go through for access to other areas of the house. Keep this in mind before you decide to make changes.

When the plumbing is roughed-in, the plumber calls for an inspection. Find the location where the plumbing inspector marks or stamps the approval, or have the plumber notify you personally when approval is obtained.

2. Concrete floor finisher

The concrete floor finishers level gravel in the basement area before placing concrete on top to cover and finish the basement floor. If there is a garage, that area could be finished at the same time. Allow a couple of days for the concrete to harden before walking on it.

3. Stair installer

As soon as the basement floor hardens, install the stairs. With split levels and two-storey designs, install the upper stairs at the same time.

4. Heating and ventilating subcontractor

Most heating and cooling units built today supply forced air. The heating and ventilating subcontractor roughs-in ducting lines from the furnace to all rooms in the house.

Air venting is supplied to the outside using separate fans and a control switch for bathrooms and the kitchen area. Air is also brought in from outside to supply the furnace.

When the furnace, ducting, and venting is in place, a thermostat wire is fed from the furnace and cooling unit through to a convenient room in the house where a control thermostatic dial fixes temperature settings for the amount of heating or cooling desired. Figure #38 illustrates a forced air venting system.

5. Electrician

The electrician comes next to install rough-in wiring and the service panel. This includes wiring for lighting, switching, and plugs, as well as wiring for motors to vent bathrooms and the kitchen area.

As power enters the house it goes directly to a main service which has a disconnect switch. The size of wire rating determines the size breaker panel distribution that the electrician installs into the house. Ask the electrician to check the maximum rating entering your house to determine which size service panel best suits your needs.

With most new construction, the size of the service entrance wire is usually capable of handling a 200 amp service, which is more than sufficient to accommodate homes built today.

When rough-in wiring work is complete, make a physical inspection of the premises; ensure that switching and fixture locations are correctly positioned. Electrical workers sometimes guess at the location for switches and fixtures which may not coincide with your plans.

All electrical work is inspected before you proceed with other interior work. Figure #39 shows a typical electrical circuit layout. As well, Appendix 13 at the back of the book contains information about placement of receptacles, outlets, and switches.

Don't proceed with insulating and vapor barrier until the electrical work is approved. The inspector might insist on seeing all wiring, and if you cover it up, you might be required to remove it. When you can't locate the inspection approval stamp, get confirmation from the electrician that all wiring is approved.

6. Cable and telephone installer

If you're planning to have cable and phone outlets in various rooms, then use a felt pen to mark out for the installer the exact location for the outlets.

7. Optional equipment installers

If optional equipment like central vacuuming, security, intercom, fireplace fans, or other features are planned then it's best to install them immediately after the electrical work is finished. Otherwise, if you wait until later you might forget and leave them out.

8. Insulation and vapor barrier installer

Next, the insulation is installed into the wall cavities. Batt insulation is the most common type used because it fits conveniently between the stud framing. Make sure the installer doesn't squash or cramp insulation or else you can lose insulation value.

After insulation, the vapor barrier is stapled to the stud walls and ceiling joists. Sheets or rolls of polyethylene film keep walls and ceilings dry and prevents outside air leaking into the interior of the house. Refer back to Figure #34 in chapter 9.

9. Permission to board

The building inspector must approve all this work before walls and ceilings are closed in. You can start the next phase before finishing this phase, as long as the electrical work is complete before exterior wall coverings are started.

FIGURE #37
HOUSE VENTING SYSTEM

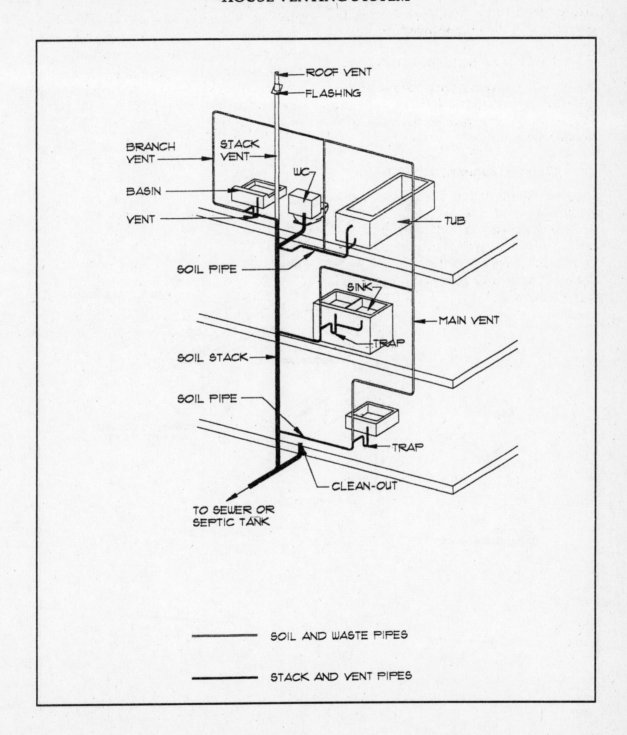

123

FIGURE #38
FORCED AIR VENTING SYSTEM

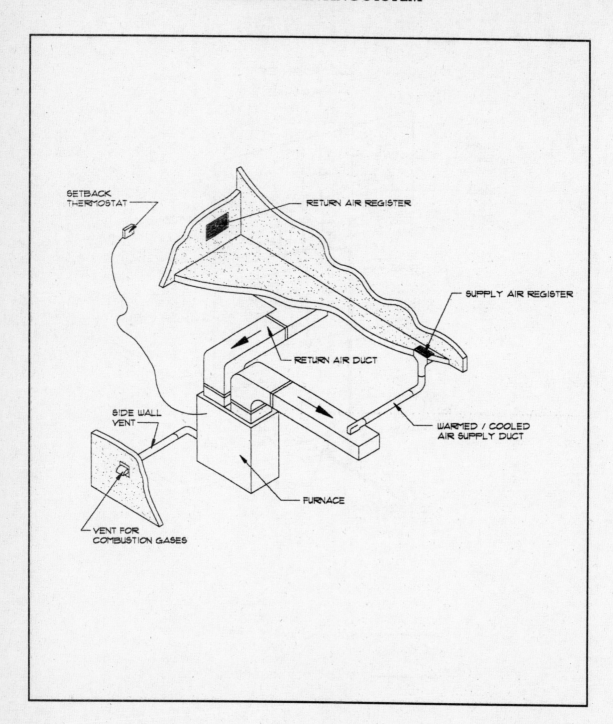

SETBACK THERMOSTAT

RETURN AIR REGISTER

SUPPLY AIR REGISTER

RETURN AIR DUCT

WARMED / COOLED AIR SUPPLY DUCT

SIDE WALL VENT

FURNACE

VENT FOR COMBUSTION GASES

FIGURE #39
CIRCUIT LAYOUT

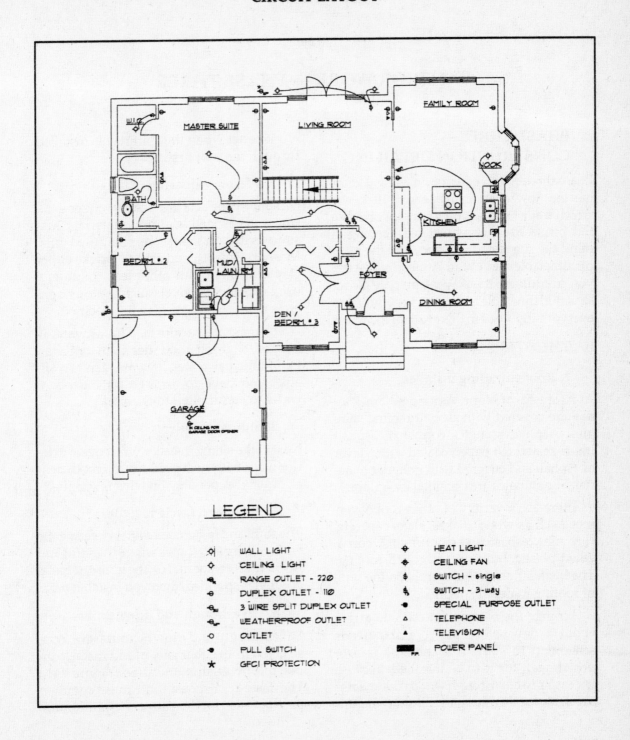

LEGEND

Symbol	Description	Symbol	Description
	WALL LIGHT		HEAT LIGHT
	CEILING LIGHT		CEILING FAN
	RANGE OUTLET - 220	$	SWITCH - single
	DUPLEX OUTLET - 110		SWITCH - 3-way
	3 WIRE SPLIT DUPLEX OUTLET		SPECIAL PURPOSE OUTLET
	WEATHERPROOF OUTLET	△	TELEPHONE
	OUTLET	▲	TELEVISION
	PULL SWITCH		POWER PANEL
✱	GFCI PROTECTION		

17

EXTERIOR WORK — PHASE THREE

a. PHASE THREE — CONSTRUCTION DETAILING

Phase three covers exterior finishing. Examine the flow chart in Appendix 10 to see which trades and suppliers are involved in this phase. Prepare a timetable, keeping in mind the suggested sequence and the sample timetable laid out in Appendix 7. After you co-ordinate the players, prepare a construction timetable and deliver a copy of it to everyone involved in this phase of the work.

b. THE STEPS

1. Roof shingling installer

At least 80% of North American homes today are covered with asphalt roofing shingles. Asphalt shingles consist of asphalt impregnated felt paper, coated with a layer of asphalt and covered with granular material. The shingles are classified by weight.

There are a variety of other roof coverings such as wood shakes, slate, concrete, clay tiles, asbestos cement, metal, corrugated plastic, built-up and rolled roofing. The installation time depends on the type of roofing material specified.

Arrange the roofing materials to arrive about a day before the roof shingler is scheduled to start. If a chimney is proposed, wait for it to be installed, because it's easier to cut through wood roof sheathing without the shingles. Flashing details work better when the chimney is installed through the roof first.

2. Masonry installer

Masonry products are used to cover exterior walls as well as siding materials. Masonry subcontractors are scheduled first. Masonry mostly consists of brick, either clay or cement. But other less commonly used masonry products such as stone, concrete block, or stucco may be specified.

For masonry products, a lot of water is needed, so it is a good idea to install a tap for municipal water. If water isn't available, you have to arrange for barrels of water to be supplied to the site.

3. Siding installer

Next is the siding installer who covers exterior walls with such products as wood, metal, or vinyl depending on what is specified.

4. Soffit and fascia installer

The soffit and fascia comes after covering the walls. Figure #40 shows where the soffit and fascia areas are located on the house. If metal or vinyl is specified, then you install it next.

5. Eavestrough and downspouts

Eavestrough and downspouts are constructed from either galvanized metal, copper, plastic, or aluminum. (See Figure #41.) The fastest, cheapest, and most common product used for this purpose is aluminum.

The eavestrough and downspouts are installed just after the soffit and fascia because eavestrough is fastened to fascia areas.

Eavestrough and downspouts provide protection from roof water rung off damaging walls. It also prevents localized erosion at the grade level near the foundation walls. Uncontrolled water run-off is a major factor contributing to a leaky basement.

6. Caulking installer

Next arrange for the caulking installers to seal all areas, especially the windows and door areas to prevent moisture and air leaking into the interior.

7. Finish carpenter

The trim or finish carpenter caps and completes all decorative details on the exterior. These jobs cover details ranging from installing shutters to completing fancy decorative trim around the main entrance doors and gable ends. Decorative details serve to identify your house's style by providing a distinguishing touch to its curb appeal.

8. Garage door installers

The garage door installation is arranged. All garage doors come in a variety of designs and are made of products ranging from wood to steel. The doors are generally assembled and installed by employees of the garage door supplier. Installation is difficult for someone without experience.

There are two types of overhead doors: a single section (swing) door and sectional overhead doors. The swing type with the single section operates on a pivot principle with a track mounted on the ceiling with rollers located at the centre top of the door.

Sectional overhead doors have rollers at each section fitted into a track at either side of the door. The overhead door has a pair of counterbalanced springs to help support the weight and make it easy to open.

Power door operators are available for most overhead doors. They operate electronically by a wall mounted button or a portable battery-powered transmitter, usually carried in a vehicle.

9. Painter

The painter comes next to finish exterior painting. All painted areas need protection from the weather. Paint keeps excess moisture out and prevents metal from rusting. If it's properly painted, it preserves wood and metal areas for several years.

10. Concrete steps and railing installer

The concrete step and railing installer follows the painter. The steps are either built on site by concrete formers or ordered from manufacturers and delivered as prefabricated steps to the entrance ways. The attached railings are made of wood or steel and are generally attached at the site.

FIGURE #40
SOFFIT AND FASCIA

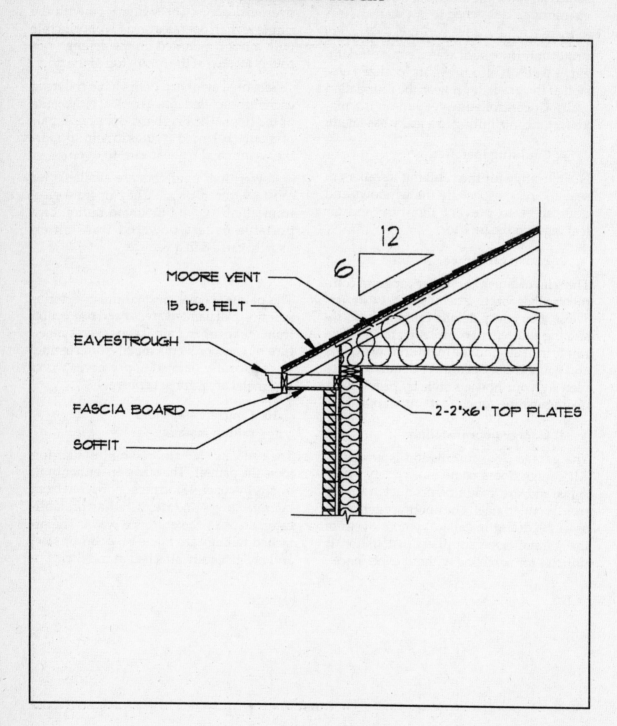

MOORE VENT

15 lbs. FELT

EAVESTROUGH

FASCIA BOARD

SOFFIT

12

6

2-2'x6' TOP PLATES

128

FIGURE #41
EAVESTROUGHS AND DOWNSPOUTS

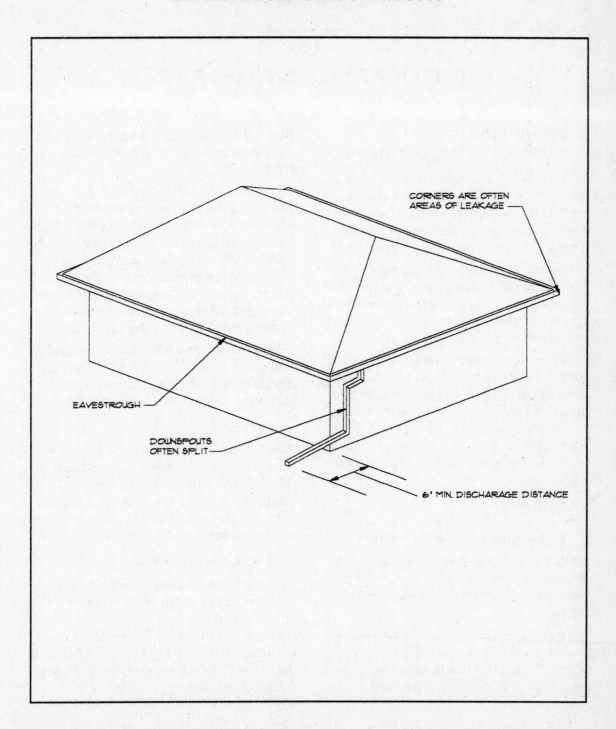

CORNERS ARE OFTEN
AREAS OF LEAKAGE

EAVESTROUGH

DOWNSPOUTS
OFTEN SPLIT

6' MIN. DISCHARAGE DISTANCE

18

INTERIOR FINISHES: PHASE FOUR

a. PHASE FOUR — CONSTRUCTION DETAILING

This phase of construction deals with all interior finishes. There are about 12 subcontractors to co-ordinate. Contact each one of them to prepare a construction timetable from the flow chart shown in Appendix 11.

Use the sample guide in Appendix 7 to set a timetable. Then carefully monitor performance because this is an area where you will potentially encounter the most problems.

When you want to re-schedule work contact the remaining subcontractors and keep them informed. Confirm the new times and make copies of revised timetables and distribute it to the remaining subcontractors as soon as possible; give them enough time to re-schedule other planned work.

b. THE STEPS

1. Boarding and coating installer

First, schedule the interior wall covering, which is the protective and decorative material applied over the stud walls and ceiling joists.

Today the majority of walls are covered with drywall (also known as gypsum wallboard). It contains two layers of tough paper. After it is nailed and screwed to the stud walls and ceilings, the joints are taped with three coats of compound applied and sanded.

Drywall board comes in a four foot width and lengths ranging in one foot increments from eight feet to 14 feet long. The drywall board for walls is half an inch thick and five-eighths inch thick for the ceilings. Some drywallers supply materials; others only supply the labor. In the latter case, obtain a list of the boarding material from the boarding subcontractor.

When the drywall surface is painted it will accept just about any sort of finishing, texturing, wallpaper and fancy decorative plastering detail such as cove moulding.

2. Painter

After boarding and taping, the painter applies prime paint and then a second coat on the walls and ceilings. The painter does not return again until the trim is ready for painting. Use semi-gloss or oil base paint on kitchen and bathroom areas.

3. Ceramic tile installer

Ceramic floor covering is installed on the kitchen and bathroom areas. If ceramic tile or resilient flooring is called for in other areas such as in the foyer, then those areas are finished at the same time. After the floors are finished, cover them to protect them against damage.

4. Cupboard and vanity installer

Next, arrange installation of the kitchen cupboards and vanities, which are usually manufactured off-site in components. They come in a variety of designs and colors. The styles have doors and fronts with raised panels, and staining reveals a clear visible grain. Others are made of material easily cleaned and that stand up to wear and tear. Nowadays, maintenance-free finishes, self-closing hidden hinges, drawers with side-mounted roller bearing suspension, and solid hardwood construction provide a durable product.

Within a day of delivery, cupboards, counter tops, and vanities should be installed and ready for the plumber to connect sinks and taps. Arrange for the installers to cut the counter top openings, but you have to obtain templates from the plumber. That way, if damage occurs while cutting, you can get them replaced without unnecessary delay.

5. Finish carpenter

The finish carpenter installs wood trim throughout the house. This includes building-out windows, installing casing around windows and doors, baseboard, interior jambs, doors, closet shelving, clothes hanger rods, built-ins, railings, fireplace finishes, attic hatch, and hardware.

The trimmer or trim supplier takes measurements and lists the trim materials needed. The materials are supplied by the trim suppliers or a lumberyard.

6. Plumber

Order the water heater, built-in dishwasher, and other built-in equipment that is connected by the plumber. Deliver those items on site just before the plumber arrives. The plumber finishes off all the plumbing by connecting waste and vent piping and hot and cold water lines.

7. Electrician

Arrange for electrical fixtures to be delivered just before the electrician arrives. Tag each fixture and designate exactly where and in which room they are to be installed. Deliver any other equipment required. The electrician ties in wiring and connects electrical equipment, electrical fixtures, plugs, switches, and covers.

8. Heating and cooling installer

The heating and cooling subcontractor then arrives to start the units. They finish installing grills and dampers and balance the air flow leading to all the rooms.

9. Phone and cable installers

Contact phone and cable companies to connect lines so that they are functional.

10. Optional equipment installers

Contact optional equipment installers to connect the equipment such as central vacuuming, security, and intercom.

11. Ceiling insulation installer

Arrange for ceiling insulation to be blown into the ceilings. This is a fast and economical method to insulate flat ceilings. The blown insulation comes in a variety of materials from cellulose to wool.

12. Hardwood floor installer

Hardwood flooring is scheduled for near the end, just before the carpet is laid. Clean and vacuum all floor areas first to reduce dust and dirt. Restrict traffic until after freshly painted floors have had an opportunity to dry properly. Then protect those areas by covering them before allowing traffic on the premises.

13. Carpet installer

Carpet flooring is left for last. Again, just before the installers arrive clean and vacuum the subfloor areas so that they don't have to lay carpet or underlay over a dirty floor.

c. INSPECTION, CLEANUP, AND PAINT TOUCH-UPS

Conduct a thorough inspection of the house. Check equipment, framing, and interior and exterior finishing (especially flashing and caulking areas). Make sure water cannot penetrate the premises and cause damage.

For more information about making inspections and maintaining your home during the first critical year, see chapter 20. A pre-occupancy inspection check should be conducted and a deficiency list prepared shortly after moving in. Forward all notices in writing to the subcontractor responsible for rectifying or completing items that are unsatisfactory or unfinished.

After everything is complete, arrange for the painter to return and complete minor repairs and paint touch-ups. The house should then be ready.

19

FINISH GRADE AND LANDSCAPING: PHASE FIVE

a. PHASE FIVE — CONSTRUCTION DETAILING

You've reached the last phase. This phase covers exterior finish grading and landscaping. It's relatively simple because you only need to co-ordinate about five or six sub-trades. See Appendix 12 for a list of the trades and suppliers involved. However, the nature of the work is seasonal, so it could take longer to complete, especially if you depend on good weather conditions.

b. THE STEPS

1. Surveyor

Call the surveyor to stake and set the final grades. The surveyor places stakes in the ground with instructions for the excavator to cut or fill to certain elevation grades by sloping and swaling the lot. The purpose is to cause surface water to drain away from the foundation walls and in specified directions.

2. Grading excavator

Using the surveyor's references as a guide, the excavator grades, cuts, fills, and shapes the ground's surface area. After final grading, the driveway, walkways, and masonry patio areas are cut down as much as six inches below grade leveled and refilled with a compacting gravel which acts as a base.

The gravelled area remains idle for a few weeks in order to naturally settle and compact. This process is accelerated by occasionally applying moderate amounts of water on the gravelled areas.

After the lot is graded, the surveyor returns and verifies the grades and ensures the ground slopes are properly draining surface water. Then the surveyor forwards a drainage certificate to the building department certifying that grading conforms to the registered grading plan or good drainage practice.

3. Optional underground equipment installers

Before sodding or seeding the optional underground equipment is installed. This refers to things such as underground sprinkler pipes and wiring.

4. Wood patio deck and fence installer

Next, wood patio decks and fencing are installed. Make sure survey stakes are visible to avoid possibly erecting structures on your neighbor's land.

5. Landscaper

Install trees, shrubbery, and plants in areas on the lot which are planned for enhancing curb appeal.

6. Driveway, walkway, and patio installer

When the gravel base is sufficiently compacted, order finish material for covering the driveway, walkways, and patio areas. Use materials such as concrete, stone, brick, or asphalt.

7. Sod or seeding installer

The sodding or seeding is left for last. Have water sprinklers available so that the sod or seeded areas are easily watered frequently. Water encourages grass to grow and take hold. Avoid cutting new grass too often and leave it about three inches high; otherwise, it burns and dies.

8. Miscellaneous

Miscellaneous items may be things such as splash pads for downspouts, mail boxes, house numbers, screens, and other items that aren't conveniently covered by specific trades.

9. Final inspection

The last step is the final building inspection. If corrections are ordered, they probably won't be serious enough to prevent you from getting an occupancy certificate if you've properly followed the steps outlined in the five phases.

At last, the house is ready to move in.

20

NEW HOME MAINTENANCE PROGRAM

After you get over the initial excitement of building and moving into your new home, you should plan to implement a periodic inspection and maintenance program. The first year after construction is critical. Some flaws and defects will become noticeable after the property is exposed to the elements and permitted to dry out.

Check the premises after a severe storm, especially the walls, roof, attic, and basement area. If you discover a problem, take corrective action immediately to minimize or prevent further damage.

A periodic maintenance program helps you to avoid major expenditures. It extends the life of all individual components and allows the systems to operate at maximum efficiency. The following are areas that need attention.

a. GROUNDS AND LANDSCAPING

1. Drainage system

Your drainage system consists of slopes, swales (shallow valleys), and possibly a catch basin for directing water away from your house and premises. Check periodically to determine if there are obstructions such as leaves or debris preventing free flow of water. Ice and snow can also create potential problems if they are not taken care of before the spring thaw.

You neighbors' landscaping plans can also adversely affect free flow of water from your premises. Before their actions get out of hand, contact your local municipality and make sure drainage regulations are enforced. If they are not, contact a lawyer for advice to solve the matter.

2. Driveway and walkways

Water collects near the edge or beneath driveway and walkways due to improper settlement. During cold weather, water freezes, causing surface areas to rise and crack. Repair, fill, and compact areas to prevent water accumulation and frost damage.

Chemical de-icers harm concrete surfaces. Asphalt, too, is particularly vulnerable when subjected to petroleum products from bicycles, motorcycles, and other vehicles. Gasoline quickly dissolves asphalt; you must wash affected areas immediately.

b. HOUSE EXTERIOR

1. Masonry work

Mortar joints between brick are not waterproof. Check those joints for shrinkage or fine cracks which are visible to the naked eye. If they are deteriorating, you should repair them to prevent further damage. Holes left open at the first course of brick (usually vertically where no mortar exists intentionally), allows moisture to escape so it doesn't build-up behind the masonry veneer walls.

Exterior stucco surfaces will show signs of hairline cracking due to shrinkage and drying which takes a year or so for the process to finish. Unfortunately this is a normal occurrence. After two years it may be necessary to apply a brush coat over the surface area.

2. Exterior cladding/siding

Exterior wood cladding is subject to moisture damage if it is continually in contact with garden sprinklers and damp shrubbery. Inspect wall surfaces for signs of paint peeling or blistering which is evidence moisture is behind the paint.

Metal and vinyl factory finished siding sometimes gets loose or blows off during severe storms. Re-fasten or repair any areas showing signs of defects.

3. Caulking

Caulking will, over time, shrink and become brittle. Periodic replacement is necessary to prevent moisture or air leaking inside the home.

4. Weatherstripping

Weatherstripping around window and door crevices reduces moisture and air transfer. It is easily damaged just from normal wear and tear. Replace weatherstripping periodically if it isn't functioning properly.

5. Outside hose connection

Carefully check to see that garden hose bibs are properly shut off and drained before cold weather sets in. Garden hoses should never be left connected to the hose bib because in the winter ice forms and damages the pipes and the hose.

6. Roof

If you maintain your roof it should last for many years. Loose, broken, or missing shingles should be replaced as soon as possible after a severe storm to prevent leakage which can cause serious damage to the interior.

Asphalt shingles are very soft during hot summer days and they are easily damaged by walking on the roof's surface. Slight color shading differences in asphalt is normal and doesn't affect its durability.

The roof vents control temperature and moisture levels in the attic area. During severe storms, snow can blow into the attic. If it accumulates and is left to melt it could cause damage.

Attic vents serve an important function and should never be obstructed or reduced in size.

7. Eavestrough and downspouts

Eavestrough is subject to clogging by debris and ice preventing proper water flow. Obstructions from leaves, paper, and surface roof particles should be removed periodically.

If ice or snow is left to accumulate in the eavestrough, it will eventually build up from temperature changes. This causes the ice to accumulate underneath shingles, and eventually, it can leak inside the house. Temporary relief is obtained by knocking ice and clearing snow from the affected areas.

8. Garage floors

It is practically impossible to prevent garage floors from cracking due to shrinkage.

Sealers applied to surface areas help but never succeed in removing the cracks completely.

c. HOUSE INTERIOR

1. Ventilation

Condensation forms on windows during the cold months. Excessive condensation is mostly due to inadequate ventilation. Serious damage occurs if the problem is left unchecked. Signs of staining, moulding, and rotting results from too much moisture.

During the first year, problems from moisture are even more acute with the house drying. Normal living habits and the number of occupants alone contribute to high levels of moisture. Be sure to acquaint yourself with the ventilation system in order to minimize moisture levels.

New homes have supplemental fans and switches in bathrooms and the kitchen area. They're designed to control local moisture and odors. By properly maintaining and operating the ventilating systems, you can minimize most moisture problems.

2. Basement

Due to shrinkage, concrete basement walls and floors often show signs of hairline cracking. A white powder sometimes appears on the surface. This is caused by salts in concrete that mix with water, and get carried to the surface as a deposit after the water evaporates in the concrete curing process. This phenomenon doesn't impair the concrete and it eventually ceases to accumulate as a deposit unless moisture is evident.

3. Framing

The framing structure consists of a wood skeleton which has a high moisture content. While wood dries, it is common to observe changes taking place within a year. Here are some results you are likely to observe the following:

(a) Drywall corners show signs of cracking and nails pop in the drywall.

(b) Small gaps become noticeable between cabinets or vanities and the walls.

(c) Minor joints open in door and window casing trim.

(d) Wood floors open between individual pieces and settlement occurs between baseboards and the floor.

(e) Squeaks develop in the floor or stairs.

(f) Thin cracks become noticeable between mouldings and wall surfaces.

Cracks and shrinkage are usually not serious. Drywall shrink cracks and nail pops are repaired easily with patching compound which is available at most lumber stores. Other cracks are repaired by using the proper caulking sealant. This is why you should finish decorating after a year or so to allow for the natural drying and settlement to occur.

4. Heating

Learn about your heating system. If the controls fail, it doesn't usually mean anything drastic is wrong, but simply an adjustment is needed.

Have your furnace serviced and cleaned annually; it is the best way to extend its life expectancy and maintain maximum efficiency. Keep heating outlets and cold air returns free from obstructions caused by carpets, draperies, and furniture.

If the furnace fails to start, check before calling for help to —

(a) make sure the switch is on,

(b) verify the thermostat setting is higher than the existing room temperature,

(c) check the electrical panel for tripped breakers, and

(d) review operating procedures in the furnace manual.

If all else fails, contact your heating and ventilating subcontractor.

Chimneys and venting need to be inspected and cleaned at least once a year. Never block air vents. If they are drafty, contact the heating and ventilating subcontractor about installing a damper.

5. Plumbing

Plumbing fixtures and pipes require commonsense care. The system isn't designed for disposing of cooking grease, fat, or similar petroleum products through the pipes. Foreign material accumulates and eventually causes the system to plug.

Throw cooking grease and solid substances out with regular garbage and occasionally flush the system with a plumbing solution to keep pipes free from sludge accumulating.

6. Septic system

The septic system requires annual inspection. Proper use and regular maintenance ensures a trouble-free performance. Septic systems are designed to handle only normal amounts of household waste water. Sending high volumes of water through the system at once causes everything to move too quickly to be properly separated and broken down. If the leaching bed is already full, waste liquids seep to the surface, or even back up into the house.

Consider composting kitchen wastes instead of using a garburator, which increases sludge accumulation. Never put petroleum products, paper, disposable diapers, sanitary tampons, condoms, rubber, plastic, or solid materials through the plumbing that leads to the septic system; dispose of those items in the garbage pick-up.

Avoid putting chemicals and fuels through the septic system because they kill bacteria which is vital for breaking down contaminants.

7. Hot water tank

Overheating and hard water are two causes of tank damage. Avoid leaving the dial in the hot position for long periods of time. Turn the temperature down or the switch off before going on vacation. When the tank stops providing hot water, check the electrical panel or the pilot light before calling an electrician or plumber.

Hot water tanks are equipped with a pressure relief valve. This safety device is designed to release if it exceeds the rated working pressure.

8. Electrical

When electrical outlets fail to work, a circuit breaker has tripped. Overloading a particular circuit, defective wiring, or defective plug connections from appliances cause circuit breakers to shut down automatically. Before calling an electrician, inspect the circuit panel to see if any breakers have tripped.

When the same circuit breaker fails repeatedly, there may be faulty wiring. Call the electrician to avoid a potential fire hazard.

9. Alarm systems

Test fire alarm systems periodically. Alarms are mandatory under building codes for new construction. Install a carbon monoxide (CO) detector which goes off if there are dangerous levels of gas from a wood burning fireplace or stove. High concentration levels of carbon monoxide causes death. If the alarm sounds, open doors, windows, and turn off ventilation systems including all exhaust fans.

d. SUMMARY

A home maintenance program is important for you to implement. Set time aside each month for checking, servicing, and maintaining your home. Follow the suggested check list in Appendix 14 for devising your own maintenance guide.

Your home is a system of subsystems that requires attention to ensure that it performs at maximum efficiency. A maintenance program ensures that those systems will actually last longer.

I hope you've gained valuable knowledge by reading this book. Your home is probably the largest investment you will ever make. To preserve your investment, maintain and look after it, and it will appreciate in value. Just imagine enjoying the comforts of home ownership while it appreciates in value.

I would like to know how you made out with your building plans. Please write to me care of Self-Counsel Press with your comments and stories.

APPENDIX 1
RESTRICTIVE COVENANTS (BUILDING SCHEMES)

The following restrictions are intended to be imposed by the vendor (developer) upon all lots within the Registered Plan as a building scheme for the Registered Plan and shall run with the lands until the _____ day of _____, 19____ , and shall be binding upon all purchasers thereof.

1. The purchaser shall not commence excavation or construction upon any lot until the purchaser has received all municipal approvals (including a building permit), obtained a grading plan, and filed with the vendor or its designated agent the following:

(a) a plot plan showing the location on the property of the proposed dwelling unit, garage, and driveway and the dimensions of all setbacks for front and side and rear yards;

(b) a set of building blueprint plans showing the proposed layout of the dwelling and garage with full specifications; and

(c) an exterior elevation plan showing the proposed exterior elevations of the dwelling unit and garage and indicating all proposed finishes and building materials (whether brick, siding, or otherwise) for the house and driveway.

All items (a), (b), and (c) must be approved in writing by the vendor (developer) or its designated agent prior to commencement of excavation or construction and all subsequent construction shall not deviate from the plot plan, the building blueprint plans, and exterior elevation plans.

2. The lot grades and elevations for the lands established by the vendor (developer) shall not be altered without the prior written consent of the vendor.

3. Notwithstanding anything contained herein to the contrary, one swimming pool will be permitted on each lot. Provided that no part of any swimming pool or the changes in the lot grading and lot elevations made in conjunction therewith, or any ancillary structures or equipment, shall be constructed, made, or placed within five feet of any lot line. In no event shall any swimming pool, grade, elevations, or swimming pool deck

extend more than four feet above the lot grade established by the vendor (developer) at the date hereof.

4. No topsoil removed in connection with grading or excavation for basements shall be sold.

5. No topsoil or subsoil removed during excavation shall be piled on the lot except during the course of construction when the same may be piled at the rear of the lot.

6. No trees presently growing on the lands shall be cut down or otherwise removed. Provided that this restriction shall not apply to prevent the cutting down or removal of any trees which may be necessary to permit the erection of a single family residence or the construction of the necessary driveway to be used in conjunction therewith.

7. No wooden fence shall be erected or maintained along any road or street upon which a house fronts.

8. No masonry wall shall be constructed along any road or street upon which a house fronts, unless the same shall have been approved in writing by the vendor, (developer).

9. No fence constructed at the rear or side of any lot shall exceed 48 inches in height unless the height of such fence is approved in writing by the vendor (developer).

10. No driveway shall be constructed on any lot unless it extends to the road curb and is provided with a flare at the curb, as required by the municipal authority having jurisdiction.

11. No outdoor clothes line other than a circular umbrella type shall be placed or maintained on the lands.

12. No camping trailer, house trailer, mobile home, or boat may be stored anywhere on the lands other than in an enclosed garage or other suitably enclosed space.

13. No refuse or garbage shall be dumped on any of the lands in the Registered Plan.

14. No building erected on the land shall be used for the purpose of any profession, trade, employment, manufacture, or any other business operation.

15. No sign, billboard, notice, or other advertising matter of any kind shall be placed on the lands or anything growing thereon, or upon or in any buildings, fences, or other things erected or placed thereon, except with the prior consent in writing of the vendor (developer),

other than one sign advertising the property for sale or rent no larger than three feet by two feet.

16. No antenna or aerial or similar structure of any nature or kind may be erected or maintained upon the lands.

17. No fence shall be erected upon the boundary between a lot zoned for single family use and a recreation park area, unless the fence shall be erected to the satisfaction of the municipal authority having jurisdiction.

18. The purchaser and any and all owners of the lot or lots within the registered plan shall not object to any application for rezoning with respect to any lots or blocks within the registered plan and this paragraph may be pleaded as a bar to any objection by the purchaser or owner(s) to any such objection to a rezoning.

19. No building shall be erected on the lands other than one detached private dwelling house suitable for the use of a single family only and may include accessory buildings either attached or detached suitable only for the use of the occupants, erected in accordance with the following specifications and constructed concurrently with the dwelling:

> (a) The house shall be either a one-storey, split-level, a one and one-half storey, or a two storey. Unless otherwise agreed in writing by the vendor (developer), the minimum area for each dwelling, exclusively of the area of the garage, shall not be less than:
>
> > (i) 1 700 square feet for a one-storey dwelling,
> >
> > (ii) 1 850 square feet for a split-level dwelling,
> >
> > (iii) 2 100 square feet for a one and one-half or a two-storey dwelling.

All of the foregoing are considered a minimum standard of the vendor (developer) and compliance with this standard shall not in any way indicate compliance with the requirements of the municipal authority having jurisdiction. Compliance with the requirements of the municipal authority shall be the sole responsibility of the owners from time to time of the lot.

> (b) The vendor (developer) shall have the right to re-enter the property for the purpose of regrading the lot in accordance with the grading plan approved by the municipal authority, which right of re-entry shall continue until such time as the subdivision is assumed by the municipal authority. On closing, the deed or transfer shall contain a right of re-entry as previously mentioned for all lots within the plan of subdivision.

20. In consideration of the vendor (developer) selling the property, the purchaser hereby covenants and agrees, on its own behalf, and on behalf of its successors and assigns, that it shall not object to a rezoning (including an official plan amendment) of any lands owned by the vendor (developer) either adjoining the subdivision within which the property is located or within one square mile of the property.

The within restrictions shall be binding and enforceable upon the owners from time to time of each of the lots within the subdivision, his or her heirs, executors, administrators, successors and assigns, and may be enforceable by the vendor (developer) its successors and assigns: but the vendor (developer) reserves unto itself its successors and assigns the right to waive or vary any of these restrictions at any time in writing without the consent in writing of the registered owner of any lot in the subdivision. Provided that the said restrictions may only be waived or varied in such minor respects as not to alter or impair the general intent of these restrictions.

It shall be presumed and such presumption may be relied upon by any subsequent purchaser or encumbrancer of the lands, that any consents or approvals of the vendor (developer), hereunder shall have been granted upon the expiration of one year from the date of completion of the construction or erection requiring such approval or consent.

In the event that any one or more of these restrictions shall be adjudged void or voidable, then only that restriction so adjudged shall be affected and the remainder of these restrictions shall remain in full force and effect and shall be interpreted as if such restriction had not been included herein.

These restrictions shall be read with all changes of number and gender required by the context.

VENDOR-(DEVELOPER)

Per: _____

PURCHASER

_____

144

APPENDIX 2
PARTICIPANTS AND SEQUENCE OF INVOLVEMENT

PARTICIPANT	SCOPE OF INVOLVEMENT
Excavator	Scrapes topsoil
Well driller	Installs well and well equipment
Surveyor	Stakes the excavation area
Excavator	Excavates hole, trenches, and lays service lines
Building inspector	Inspects soils condition
Concrete footings former	Cribs and pours footings
Surveyor	Sets elevations for digging and marks corners for foundation walls
Foundation installer	Constructs foundation walls
Dampproofer	Installs dampproof material on walls
Water shield installer	Wraps waterproof material around foundation walls
Weeping tile installer	Installs weeping tile and gravel, including levelling gravel in basement
Building inspector	Inspects for granting permission to backfill
Excavator	Backfills foundation to grade level
Septic installer	Installs sewage disposal system

Health inspector	Inspects sewage disposal system
Framing material supplier	Supplies and delivers framing materials
Window and door supplier	Supplies and delivers windows and doors
Truss manufacturer	Supplies and delivers roof truss members (optional)
Framing installer	Frames house structure, installs windows and doors and basement strapping
Building inspector	Inspects framing structure
Plumber	Installs base plumbing and rough-in plumbing
Plumbing inspector	Inspects base plumbing and house rough-in plumbing
Roofing installer	Installs shingles and flashing
Concrete floor installer	Installs concrete basement floor and concrete garage floors
Heating and ventilating installer	Supplies and delivers furnace and (optional) air conditioning, rough-in ducting and venting
Heating inspector	Inspects heating and (optional) air conditioning systems, including venting and ducting
Electrician	Installs service panel and rough-in wiring
Electrical inspector	Inspects electrical wiring and service panel

Note: Confirm plumbing, heating, and electrical inspections are finished and approved before commencing with other interior finishes.

Painter	Prime paints exterior areas
Clad or veneer supplier	Supplies masonry or siding materials for exterior walls

Masonry veneer installer	Installs brick or other masonry materials for exterior walls
Siding installer	Installs siding materials for exterior walls
Interior systems rough-in installers (optional)	Rough-in telephone, cable, security, central vacuuming, and intercom
Insulating and vapor barrier installer	Supplies and installs insulation and vapor barrier
Boarding and taping installer	Supplies and installs drywall board, taping and sanding to make ready for paint (for plaster-supplies and installs plaster board, surface putty coats to make ready for paint)
Painter	Paints interior walls and ceilings
Trim supplier	Supplies and delivers trimming material, shelving, and hardware
Trim carpenter	Installs trim material
Painter	Finishes interior painting
Resilient and ceramic floor installer	Installs flooring on kitchens, bathrooms and foyer-ceramic on walls in shower stalls and bath areas
Kitchen cupboard and vanity supplier and installer	Supplies and installs kitchen cupboards, countertops, and vanities
Plumbing fixture supplier	Supplies and delivers plumbing fixtures
Plumber	Finishes plumbing and installs plumbing fixtures
Electrical fixture supplier	supplies and delivers electrical fixtures
Electrician	Finishes electrical and installs electrical fixtures

Heating and ventilating	Finishes heating and air conditioning
Optional systems installer	Finishes central vacuuming, intercom, security, etc.
Eavestrough and down spout installer	Supplies and installs eavestrough and downspouts
Surveyor	Sets elevation grades for drainage
Excavator	Cuts and slopes lot to elevation grades, place topsoil and gravel base
Surveyor	Confirms, certifies grades and prepares survey report
Underground service	Supplies and installs underground wiring or supplies and installs underground water sprinkler pipes
Driveway and walkway installer	Supplies and installs surface finish areas for driveway and or walkways
Landscape installer	Supplies and installs shrubbery, sod, or seeding
Fence and decking installer	Supplies and installs fence and decking
Hardwood floor installer	Supplies, installs, and finishes hardwood flooring
Carpet installer	Supplies and installs underlay and carpet
Trim carpenter	Finishes trim, hardware, and shelving
Painter	Finishes and touches up
Building inspector	Final inspection and certificate of occupancy

APPENDIX 3
INVITATION TO BID — SUBCONTRACTOR

Owner-builder   Subcontractor

Your full name _____   Name_____

Address _____   Address_____

Phone number _____   Phone number_____

Job location _____

Address _____

Indicate the amount of lead time required before commencing the work.
(lead time_____)

Indicate the approximate amount of time to perform the work. If possible, break down work functions into allotted times.

_____

_____

_____

It is acknowledged that this invitation and the terms contained herein shall form part of the contract terms unless these terms are specifically excluded in writing and agreed to by all parties.

SCOPE OF THE WORK

You are invited to submit your bid or quotation for the following work on the condition that the terms as outlined in this invitation are automatically included as part of the contract terms:

(examine Appendix 2 for an example; see excavator's scope of involvement)

(sample)
"Scrape top soil, excavate hole, trench and lay service lines, backfill foundation to grade level, cut and slope lot to elevation grades, place top soil and gravel base"

Without limiting the generality of the above, all work shall be performed in accordance with the plans, specifications, grading, and site plan which are filed, amended, and approved by the municipal authority having jurisdiction. The subcontractor acknowledges having inspected all building documents before submitting a bid or quotation.

SUPPLY OF MATERIALS
The subcontractor shall supply the following materials (list the materials if applicable):

_____

_____

_____

_____

The owner-builder shall supply the following materials (list the materials if applicable):

_____

_____

_____

_____

SPECIAL PERMITS
The subcontractor agrees to assume responsibility for obtaining and paying for the cost of special permits covered by the above described work (if any). The subcontractor agrees that payments may be suspended until the work is inspected and approved by the authority having jurisdiction.

HOLDBACK
The subcontractor acknowledges the right of the owner-builder to retain a holdback from advances or from the final payment provided the holdback is in compliance with the construction or mechanic's lien legislation prescribed by provincial law.

WORKERS' COMPENSATION

The subcontractor agrees to maintain workers' compensation coverage for all persons in their control working on the owner-builder's job site as required by provincial law.

PRICE

The price is $_____ based on a fixed sum for the work. Or, alternatively the price is based on (if price is determined according to a formula provide a definition)

_____

_____

_____

_____

UNFORESEEN CHANGES

No extra charges are payable for additional work or changes made after the contract is finalized unless a price is agreed to in writing by all parties.

CLEAN UP

On completion of each phase of the work the subcontractor shall leave the premises in a clean and tidy condition. If the premises are left with debris, garbage, or fill material lying around, the owner-builder shall be permitted to back charge a reasonable amount for clean up and removal.

DAMAGE TO THE PREMISES

The subcontractor shall take all necessary steps to protect the job site from damage. If damage occurs the subcontractor shall be responsible for the cost of repairing or replacing all property damaged by the subcontractor, their employees, agents, or invitees.

PAYMENT TERMS

The terms of payment are as follows

_____

_____

_____

_____

_____

GUARANTEE

The subcontractor agrees to guarantee work and materials for _____ (years) from the date of completion of the contract. If the date of completion is disputed then unless otherwise proved the date of completion is presumed to correspond to the date when the final payment is due and payable.

ADDITIONAL TERMS

Note: Add additional terms as are necessary from negotiations to protect your interest.

DATED at _____ this _____ day of _____ 19____ .

_____
SUBCONTRACTOR

APPENDIX 4
INVITATION TO BID — MATERIAL SUPPLIER

Owner-builder   Material supplier

Your full name _____   Name _____
Address _____   Address _____
Phone number_____   Phone number _____

Job location _____

Address _____

Indicate the amount of lead time required in order to have the materials delivered on time. (lead time _____)

The material supplier acknowledges having inspected the plans and specifications.

MATERIALS REQUESTED FOR SUPPLY AND DELIVERY

You are invited to submit your quotation or bid for the following:

(See Appendix 2 for a sample supply and delivery of windows and doors according to the plans and specifications or as otherwise agreed to by the parties) on the condition that the terms as outlined in this invitation are automatically included as part of the contract terms.

UNAUTHORIZED DELIVERY

When materials are delivered before they are requested by the owner/builder or the designated agent, the material supplier shall assume responsibility to protect those materials against theft or damage until they are incorporated into the house.

DELIVERING DAMAGE OR DEFECTIVE MATERIALS

The material supplier agrees to pick up defective or damaged materials within 48 hours of notice; otherwise the materials are at the risk of the supplier.

DAMAGE TO THE PREMISES

The supplier shall take all necessary steps to protect the job site by indemnifying the owner/builder against all damage caused during deliveries by the supplier, their employees, agents, or invitees.

GUARANTEE

The material supplier agrees to guarantee all materials against defects and workmanship for a period of _____ (years) from the date of delivery.

PRICE

The price is $ _____

PAYMENT TERMS

The terms of payment are _____

_____

_____

HOLDBACK

The material supplier acknowledges the right of the owner-builder to retain a holdback provided that the holdback is in compliance with the construction or mechanic's lien legislation prescribed by provincial law.

ADDITIONAL TERMS

Note: Add additional terms as needed.

DATED at _____ this _____ day of _____ 19____ .

_____
MATERIAL SUPPLIER

APPENDIX 5
BUILDING BUDGET ANALYSIS

COST CLASSIFICATION	ESTIMATED COST	TOTAL	ACTUAL COST	ACTUAL TOTAL	DIFFERENCE
1. GENERAL ITEMS					
1. Drawings, etc.					
2. Municipal charges					
3. Survey fees					
4. Lawyer fees					
5. Administration fees					
6. Insurance fees					
7. General labor		_____		_____	_____
2. WELL DRILLING		_____		_____	_____
3. EXCAVATING					
1. Strip top soil					
2. Excavate hole					
3. Backfill					
4. Final grade					
5. Walkways & driveway					
6. Materials		_____		_____	_____
4. FOOTINGS AND FOUNDATION					
1. Place footings					
2. Material costs					
3. Construct foundation					
4. Materials for foundation		_____		_____	_____

COST CLASSIFICATION	ESTIMATED		ACTUAL		DIFFERENCE
	COST	TOTAL	COST	TOTAL	
5. DAMPPROOFING					
1. Dampproofing					
2. Drainage shield		———		———	———
6. WEEPING TILE AND GRAVEL					
1. Labor tile and gravel					
2. Labor gravel in base					
3. Materials		———		———	———
7. FRAMING MATERIALS					
1. Lumber					
2. Windows and doors					
3. Steel beams					
4. Roof trusses					
5. Misc. materials		———		———	———
8. FRAMING LABOR		———		———	———
9. ROOFING					
1. Labor					
2. Materials		———		———	———
10. CONCRETE FLOOR					
1. Labor					
2. Materials		———		———	———
11. MECHANICAL SYSTEMS					
1. Plumbing					
2. Plumbing fixtures					

COST CLASSIFICATION	ESTIMATED COST TOTAL	ACTUAL COST TOTAL	DIFFERENCE
3. Heating			
4. Cooling (A/C)			
5. Electrical			
6. Misc. materials			
7. Phone			
8. Cable			
9. Central vacuum			
10. Security			
11. Inter-com			
12. Misc. equipment	———	———	———
12. INSULATION AND VAPOR BARRIER			
1. Labor			
2. Materials	———	———	———
13. CEILING AND WALL BOARD			
1. Labor			
2. Materials	———	———	———
14 EXTERIOR WALLS			
1. Masonry labor			
2. Masonry materials			
3. Fireplace			
4. Siding labor			
5. Siding materials			
6. Soffit & fascia			
7. Misc. materials	———	———	———
15. EAVESTROUGH & DOWNSPOUTS	———	———	———

COST CLASSIFICATION	ESTIMATED		ACTUAL		DIFFERENCE
	COST	TOTAL	COST	TOTAL	
16. ROOF FLASH AND CAULKING		———		———	———
17. SEPTIC AND FIELD BED		———		———	———
18. CEILING INSULATION		———		———	———
19. CERAMIC TILE		———		———	———
20. FLOOR COVERINGS					
1. Resilient flooring					
2. Ceramic flooring					
3. Hardwood flooring					
4. Carpet					
5. Misc. labor		———		———	———
21. KITCHEN CUPBOARDS		———		———	———
22. BUILT-IN APPLIANCES					
1. Water heater					
2. Built-in appliances					
3. Connection charges		———		———	———
23. HARDWARE, TRIM, ETC.					
1. Trim materials					
2. Hardware					
3. Shelving					
4. Railing					

COST CLASSIFICATION	ESTIMATED		ACTUAL		DIFFERENCE
	COST	TOTAL	COST	TOTAL	
5. Mirrors					
6. Misc.		_____		_____	_____
24. TRIMMING CARPENTER		_____		_____	_____
25. PAINTING & DECORATING					
1. Labor					
2. Materials					
3. Misc.		_____		_____	_____
26. ELECTRICAL FIXTURES		_____		_____	_____
27. LANDSCAPING					
1. Sod or seeding					
2. Shrubbery, plants					
3. Patio					
4. Fencing					
5. Walkway					
6. Driveway		_____		_____	_____
28. EXTRAS & OTHERS		_____		_____	_____
29. BUILDING COST ESTIMATE	$_____				
30. LAND COST	$_____		$_____		
31. PROJECT ESTIMATE TOTAL	$_____				
32. ACTUAL PROJECT TOTAL			$_____		
33. DIFFERENCE (30 - 31)					$_____

APPENDIX 6
CMHC GUIDE TO PERCENTAGE COMPLETION OF HOUSES

Actual %	%	Item
_____	16	Excavation, foundation, beams, columns, joists, sub-floor
_____	22	Backfill, framing, sheathing, roof, roughed-in electrical, roughed-in plumbing, insulation, vapor barrier
_____	2	Roughed-in heating
_____	3	Exterior doors and windows
_____	12	Exterior finish
_____	3	Basement floor
_____	5	Heating equipment
_____	2	Interior doors
_____	8	Interior wall and ceiling finish
_____	3	Finish floor coverings
_____	1	Complete electrical (including fixtures)
_____	4	Complete plumbing (including fixtures)
_____	11	Finish carpentry
_____	5	Painting
_____	3	Site works and improvements
_____	100	Total percentage complete

Note: In cases where "items" are partially completed, the examiner may adjust the % related to such items proportionate to the actual completion level of these items. As an example, if "Exterior Finish" was 50% completed, 6% could be added to the Total Percentage Complete for advancing purposes. If the same item was almost completed, 10% would be a reasonable percentage to be added to the total.

APPENDIX 7
CONSTRUCTION TIMETABLE

DAY	ITEM CHECK	JOB ITEM	DATE REQUEST	DATE START	DATE COMPLETE
21 DAYS PRIOR		Receive mortgage approval Contact trades and material suppliers in phase one (see Appendix 8) Contact lawyer re: mortgage particulars Apply for building permit			
14 DAYS PRIOR		Drill or dig well			
7 DAYS PRIOR		Pick up building permit Order steel beams Order roof trusses Order windows and doors Set up framing loads Deliver timetable to trades and material suppliers for phase one			
3 DAYS PRIOR		Scrape top soil			
2 DAYS PRIOR		Underground locates for hydro, water, gas, cable, and phone			
1 DAY PRIOR		Surveyor stakes lot			
DAY 1		Excavator trenches service lines and excavates hole			
DAY 2		Building inspector inspects soils — personally attend with inspector			

DAY	ITEM CHECK	JOB ITEM	DATE REQUEST	DATE START	DATE COMPLETE
DAY 3		Concrete former cribs footings and pours concrete			
DAY 4		Gravel placed in basement area and leveled			
DAY 5		Surveyor pins location for foundation walls			
DAY 6		Foundation installer			
DAY 9		Dampproof installer			
DAY 10		Water shield installer			
DAY 11		Weeping tile and gravel			
DAY 12		Building inspector — for backfill personally attend with inspector			
DAY 13		Deliver first lumber load and nails; deliver steel beams			
DAY 14		Start framing			
DAY 15		Contact trades and material suppliers for phase two (see Appendix 9)			
DAY 16		Deliver second lumber load			
DAY 20		Deliver third lumber load			
DAY 21		Deliver roof trusses			
DAY 23		Deliver windows and doors			
DAY 27		Deliver timetable to trades and suppliers for second phase			
DAY 28		Building inspection - framing personally attend with inspector			
DAY 29		Install septic tank and field bed (if no municipal sewage available)			

DAY	ITEM CHECK	JOB ITEM	DATE REQUEST	DATE START	DATE COMPLETE
DAY 30		Secure premises and "no trespassing signs"			

END OF PHASE 1

DAY	ITEM CHECK	JOB ITEM	DATE REQUEST	DATE START	DATE COMPLETE
DAY 31		Install underground base plumbing and plumbing rough-in			
DAY 32		Plumbing inspection: contact trades and material suppliers in phase three (see Appendix 10)			
DAY 33		Pour basement floor			
DAY 34		Build stairs			
DAY 35		Install stairs			
DAY 36		Rough-in heating and cooling: deliver timetable to trades and material suppliers for phase three			
DAY 40		Rough-in wiring and electrical service			
DAY 42		Inspections: conduct a personal inspection			
DAY 43		Cable and phone rough-in			
DAY 44		Optional equipment rough-in			
DAY 45		Install insulation			
DAY 46		Install vapor barrier Building inspection, attend with inspector			

END OF PHASE 2

DAY	ITEM CHECK	JOB ITEM	DATE REQUEST	DATE START	DATE COMPLETE
DAY 46		Deliver roofing materials			
DAY 47		Install roofing shingles			

DAY	ITEM CHECK	JOB ITEM	DATE REQUEST	DATE START	DATE COMPLETE
DAY 48		Deliver masonry materials (arrange for water)			
DAY 49		Start masonry work			
DAY 50		Contact trades and material suppliers in phase four (see Appendix 11)			
DAY 59		Deliver siding materials			
DAY 60		Start siding work			
DAY 62		Install flashing and caulking			
DAY 63		Deliver timetable to trades and material suppliers for phase four			
DAY 64		Install soffit and fascia			
DAY 66		Paint exterior			
DAY 68		Install eavestrough and downspouts			
DAY 69		Install exterior decorative detailing; assemble and install garage doors			
DAY 70		Install concrete steps and railing			
END OF PHASE 3					
DAY 71		Deliver drywall board, tape, and compound			
DAY 72		Start boarding			
DAY 76		Start taping			
DAY 90		Deliver paint materials			
DAY 91		Start painting			
DAY 97		Install ceramic and resilient flooring - kitchen and bathrooms			

DAY	ITEM CHECK	JOB ITEM	DATE REQUEST	DATE START	DATE COMPLETE
DAY 99		Install cupboards and vanities			
DAY 100		Deliver trim, doors, and hardware			
DAY 101		Start trimming			
DAY 105		Contact trades and material suppliers for phase five (see Appendix 12)			
DAY 107		Finish painting and staining			
DAY 108		Deliver water heater and appliances			
DAY 109		Finish plumbing, install plumbing fixtures			
DAY 110		Deliver electrical fixtures			
DAY 111		Finish electrical and install fixtures			
DAY 112		Deliver timetable to trades and suppliers for phase 5			
DAY 113		Connect furnace and air conditioning connect phone and cable Connect optional equipment			
DAY 114		Install hardwood flooring			
DAY 115		Paint hardwood floors			
DAY 118		Install carpet			
END OF PHASE 4					
DAY 119		Set final grades			
DAY 120		Complete final grading			
DAY 121		Final grading certificate			
DAY 122		Install optional undergrounds			
DAY 123		Start wood deck and fencing			

DAY	ITEM CHECK	JOB ITEM	DATE REQUEST	DATE START	DATE COMPLETE
DAY 125		Install trees and plantings			
DAY 134		Start walkway and driveway			
DAY 136		Install miscellaneous items			
DAY 137		Final inspection and clean up			

APPENDIX 8
FLOW CHART FOR PHASE ONE —
BASIC STRUCTURE AND SERVICES

Well driller	(If municipal water is unavailable)
Building permit	Permission to commence construction
Excavator	Scrapes top soil
Surveyor	Stakes excavation
Excavator	Trenches service lines; excavates hole
Building inspector	Inspects soil
Concrete former	Cribs and pours footings; installs and levels gravel in basement
Surveyor	Pins foundation walls
Foundation installer	Constructs foundation walls
Dampproof installer	Dampproofs foundation walls
Water shield installer	Wraps waterproof material around foundation
Weeping tile and gravel installer	Installs weeping tile and gravel
Building inspector	Inspects for giving approval to backfill
Framing material supplier	Delivers lumber and nails
Steel fabricator	Delivers steel beams

Truss manufacturer	Delivers truss members
Framing installer	Constructs wood frame structure
Window and door supplier	Delivers windows and doors
Building inspector	Inspects framing structure
Personal inspection	Inspects for backing, change orders, and quality
Septic tank installer	Installs septic tank and field bed (if no municipal sewage available)
Security	Secures premises and installs "no trespassing signs"

APPENDIX 9
FLOW CHART FOR PHASE TWO — INTERIOR ROUGH-INS

Plumber	Installs underground plumbing in basement; roughs-in plumbing
Concrete floor finisher	Installs concrete basement floor; installs garage concrete floors
Stair installer	Installs stairs to all levels
Heating and ventilating installer	Installs heating and cooling rough-ins
Electrical wiring installer	Installs service panel and rough wiring
Cable and phone installer	Installs rough-in cable and phone lines
Optional equipment installers	Installs rough-in central vac, security, intercom, fireplace fans, and built-in speakers
Insulation and vapor barrier installer	Installs insulation and vapor barrier
Building inspector	Inspects for permission to board in

APPENDIX 10
FLOW CHART FOR PHASE THREE —
ROOF SHINGLING, EXTERIOR WALL COVERINGS,
GARAGE DOORS, STEPS, AND RAILINGS

Roofing supplier	Supplies roofing materials and shingles
Roofing installer	Installs roofing shingles
Masonry installer	Supplies masonry materials
Siding supplier	Supplies siding such as aluminum, vinyl, wood, etc.
Siding installer	Installs siding
Soffit and fascia installer	Installs soffit and fascia
Eavestrough and down spout installer	Installs eavestrough and down spouts
Flashing and caulking installer	Installs flashing and caulking to make water and/or airtight
Finish carpenter	Installs exterior decorative detailing
Garage door installer	Assembles and installs garage doors
Painter	Installs exterior painting
Concrete step and railing installer	Installs concrete steps and railing

APPENDIX 11
FLOW CHART FOR PHASE FOUR — INTERIOR FINISHES

Drywall board supplier	Supplies drywall boarding, taping, and compound
Boarding and taping installer	Installs drywall board and taping
Painting supplier	Supplies painting materials
Painter	Paints interior walls, ceilings, trim, and doors (three coats)
Resilient and ceramic floor supplier and installer	Supplies and installs ceramic and resilient flooring, ceramic in shower stalls, bathtub surround, and bath fixtures
Kitchen cupboard and vanity supplier	Supplies and installs kitchen cupboards, vanities, and countertops
Trim supplier	Supplies trim material, hardware, doors, railing, and shelving
Finish carpenter	Installs trim, hardware, doors, shelves, and railing
Plumber	Finishes plumbing and installs plumbing fixtures
Electrician	Connects wires, ties-in appliances, installs plugs, switches, covers, and electrical fixtures
Heating and cooling installer	Connects furnace and air conditioning, installs dampers, covers, and adjusts air flow
Phone and cable installers	Installs plugs, covers, and connects phone and cable

Optional equipment installer	Connects optional equipment such as central vac and security
Hardwood flooring installer	Installs and paints hardwood flooring
Carpet installers	Supplies and installs underlay and carpeting

APPENDIX 12
FLOW CHART FOR PHASE FIVE —
FINISH GRADE AND LANDSCAPING

Surveyor	Sets final grades
Grading excavator	Completes final grading
Surveyor	Final grading certificate
Underground installer	Installs underground optional equipment
Deck and fence installer	Installs wood deck and fencing
Landscaper	Installs trees, shrubbery, and plants
Driveway & walkway installer	Installs covering for driveway, walkway, and patio
Sod or seeding installer	Installs sod or seeding
Miscellaneous installers	Installs mail box, numbers, etc.
Building inspector	Final inspection

APPENDIX 13
PLACEMENT OF RECEPTACLES, OUTLETS, AND SWITCHES

AREA	WALL RECEPTACLES	USES	REQUIREMENTS FOR SPECIAL OUTLETS	PERMANENT LIGHTING	SWITCHES
GENERAL	Maximum distance 12 ft. apart	Clock, radio, TV, iron, lamps	Portable A/C	Ceiling or walls	Single beside entry door 3-way for more than one entry
BEDRM(S)	Maximum distance 12 ft. apart	Electric blanket, clock, radio, or TV	Portable A/C	Ceiling or walls	Beside entry door
KITCHEN	Split duplex receptacles at counters	Toaster, clock, microwave, blender	Range, dishwasher, fridge, garburator	Ceiling, over sink, light & fan over stove	3-way beside each entry door
LAUNDRY	Duplex recpt at table ht. washer on separate circuit	Iron, sewing machine	Dryer	Ceiling	Beside entry door
BATHROOM	Beside entry counter GFCI protection min. 3 ft. from shower or bath	Dryer, razor, toothbrush	Vent fan, heat lamp	Ceiling & beside mirror	Beside entry door
HALLWAY & STAIRS	Max. distance 12 ft. apart	Vacuum cleaner, polisher		Ceiling or wall	3-way to control at both ends
CLOSET	None allowed	None allowed	None allowed	Ceiling	Preferably door operated
FAMILY OR REC ROOM	Max. 12 ft., apart	TV, computer, musical	Supplement heating	Ceiling or walls	Beside entry

AREA	WALL RECEPTACLES	USES	REQUIREMENTS FOR SPECIAL OUTLETS	PERMANENT LIGHTING	SWITCHES
UTILITY ROOM	Furnace, freezer, work area	Power tools, freezer, humidifier	Heating equip., water heater, central air	Ceiling	Beside entry
PORCH & PATIO	Weatherproof	Radio, TV, lawn mower, barbecue	GFCI protection	Outside porch	Inside porch door
GARAGE	One for general use	Block heater, work bench	Garage door opener	Ceiling for interior, wall for exterior	Inside door

APPENDIX 14
ANNUAL HOME MAINTENANCE GUIDE

	19__	19__	19__

JANUARY

1. Remove snow and ice — roof overhang and vents
2. Check and clean furnace filter and HRV
3. Check water heater
4. Clean humidifier
5. Clean range hood filter

FEBRUARY

1. Remove snow and ice — Roof overhang and vents
2. Check and clean furnace filter and HRV
3. Check and clean fireplace and chimney
4. Check inside walls, ceiling, and floor surfaces
5. Clean humidifier

MARCH

1. Remove snow and ice — roof overhang and vents
2. Check and clean furnace and HRV
3. Conduct annual safety check
   Door locks
   Window locks
   Smoke alarms
   CO alarm
   Potential hazards
4. Check attic
5. Check sump pump (if installed)
6. Clean humidifier
7. Inspect basement and crawl spaces
8. Check water surface drainage for ponding

	19__	19__	19__

APRIL
1. Clean eavestrough and downspouts
2. Check furnace and HRV
3. Clean humidifier
4. Check for loose or damaged roofing
5. Check for loose or damaged siding
6. Check driveway and walkways for frost damage
7. Check water heater
8. Check for and repair landscaping settlement
9. Clean range hood filter

MAY
1. Check windows and screens
2. Repair or replace weatherstripping
3. Check septic system (if installed)
4. Check air conditioning
5. Fertilize lawns
6. Inspect fencing

JUNE
It's your month off!
No regular maintenance checks needed at this time of year.

JULY
1. Air out damp basement
2. Check exhaust fans
3. Check water heater

AUGUST
1. Air out damp basement
2. Clean rangehood filter
3. Check smoke alarm
4. Check CO alarm

SEPTEMBER

1. Service humidifier, furnace, and HRV
2. Inspect and clean fireplace and chimney
3. Check basements and crawl space
4. Plant new lawn areas
5. Fertilize lawn
6. Check and replace caulking
7. Check garage doors and tracks
8. Check exterior finishes

OCTOBER

1. Check windows and screens
2. Check smoke and CO alarms
3. Check roof shingles, vents, and flashing
4. Check septic system
5. Winterize landscaping and remove leaves
6. Clean eavestrough and downspouts
7. Clean water heater
8. Clean humidifier

NOVEMBER

1. Clean range hood
2. Check for condensation and humidity
3. Check ventilating systems
4. Fill floor drain trap if necessary

DECEMBER

1. Remove snow and ice — roof overhang and vents
2. Check furnace filter and HRV
3. Clean humidifier

19__	19__	19__

APPENDIX 15
MODEL AGREEMENT

THIS AGREEMENT DATED THIS _____ DAY OF _____ 19 ___

BETWEEN:

OWNER/BUILDER _____
(full name)

_____

_____   _____
(address)   (phone no.)

-and-

SUBCONTRACTOR _____
(full name)

_____

_____   _____
(address)   (phone no.)

JOB LOCATION_____
(address)

The owner/builder agrees to hire the subcontractor on the following terms and conditions:

1. ACKNOWLEDGMENT

The subcontractor acknowledges having inspected all relevant documents including the house plans, specifications, and site plan.

2. RESPONSIBILITY FOR MATERIALS (delete inappropriate clauses)

The owner/builder is responsible for supplying all materials. Or, the subcontractor is responsible for supplying all materials. If materials are shared between both parties then

provide: The subcontractor is responsible for supplying the following materials [list them] and the owner/builder is responsible for supplying the following materials [list them].

3. COMMENCEMENT OF THE WORK

The subcontractor shall commence the work within _____ days of receiving notice to commence from the owner/builder. If the subcontractor fails to commence the work within the time provided without receiving an extension, the owner/builder is at liberty to hire another subcontractor to perform the work. Time in all respects shall be of the essence.

4. SCOPE OF THE WORK

The work entails the following [see Appendix 2] _____
_____
 in accordance with the house plans, specifications, and site plan.

The subcontractor furnishes all labor, tools, scaffolding, water, electricity, heat, other services, and supervision for carrying out the work according to the house plans, specifications, and site plan. Notwithstanding the house plans, specifications, and site plan, all work is to be carried out in accordance with applicable codes and laws having jurisdiction and the price stated herein covers for changes needed to comply with those laws.

All work shall be carried out diligently in a good and workmanlike manner.

The subcontractor warrants all work and materials pursuant to this agreement for a period of .... year(s) from completion. When the date of completion is in dispute the date is presumed to correspond to the date when final payment became payable unless otherwise proved.

The subcontractor shall protect work, owner's property, and surrounding properties from damage occasioned by the construction and completion of the work.

The subcontractor is responsible for cleaning up and removing all debris from the site before leaving the premises.

This agreement is contingent upon strikes, accidents, or delays beyond the subcontractor's control.

5. EXTRAS OR CREDITS

No extra charges are payable by the owner/builder for additional work performed and no credits are payable to the owner/builder after signing the contract unless a price for the extras or credits is agreed to by both parties in writing.

6. PRICE (includes all taxes except GST)

The price is $_____ based on a fixed sum for the work. Or, the price is based on the following formula _____

Extra is added for the following; [list with the applicable dollar amounts]. Except as listed in the preceding the subcontractor waives the right to charge further extras for work performed unless specifically agreed to in writing by the parties.

Payment shall be made within _____ days from the date of receiving an invoice after the completion of the work in accordance with the terms and conditions of this agreement.

7. HOLDBACK

The subcontractor acknowledges the right of the owner/builder to retain a holdback for construction or mechanic's liens as specified by provincial law.

8. SPECIAL PERMITS

The subcontractor is responsible for obtaining and paying for all special permits. This includes the responsibility for the subcontractor to request inspections and obtain approvals for the work covered by the permit before submitting an account for payment of an advance or the price.

9. WORKERS' COMPENSATION

The subcontractor shall maintain workers' compensation coverage for all persons in their control working on the owner/builder's job site as required by provincial law and if requested will provide evidence of coverage in good standing.

10. PUBLIC LIABILITY AND PROPERTY DAMAGE

The subcontractor agrees to provide proof of builder's risk insurance in effect to the amount of $ 1 000 000 liability prior to commencing the work, including general liability insurance and automobile liability insurance.

The above price, specifications, terms, and conditions are satisfactory and are hereby accepted.

This agreement shall be construed under the laws of the Province of _____.
This agreement supersedes all prior communications, representations, and agreements and there are no other terms or conditions except as provided in this agreement.

SIGNATURES

_____

(owner/builder)

_____

(subcontractor)

APPENDIX 16
METRIC UNITS FOR COMMON USE
(Conversion factors approximate)

QUANTITY	METRIC UNIT AND SYMBOL	CUSTOMARY TO METRIC UNITS	METRIC TO CUSTOMARY UNITS
LENGTH	MILLIMETRE (mm)	1 in = 25.4 mm	1 mm = 0.03940 in
	CENTIMETRE (cm)	1 in = 2.54 cm	1 cm = 0.394 in
		1 ft = 30.5 cm	
	METRE (m)	1 yd = 0.914 m	1 m = 3.28 ft
	KILOMETRE (km)	1 mi = 1.61 km	1 km = 0.62 mi
WEIGHT (MASS)	GRAM (g)	1 oz = 28.3 g	1 g = 0.0353 oz
	KILOGRAM (km)	1 lb = 454 g	1 kg = 2.2 lb
	TONNE (t)	1 ton = 1.02	1 t = 0.98 long ton
AREA	SQ. CENT (cm^2)	$1 in^2 = 6.45 cm^2$	$1 cm^2 = 0.155 in^2$
	SQUARE METRE (m^2)	$1 ft^2 = 929 cm^2$	$1 m^2 = 10.8 ft^2$
	HECTARE (ha)	1 acre = 0.405 ha	1 ha = 2.47 acres
	SQ. KILOMETRE (km^2)	$1 mi^2 = 2.59 km^2$	$1 km^2 = 0.386 mi^2$
VOLUME	CUBIC CENT (cm^3)	$1 in^3 = 16.4 cm^3$	$1 cm^3 = 0.061 in^3$
	CUBIC METRE (m^3)	$1 ft^3 = 28\,300 cm^3$	$35.3 ft^3$
		$1 yd^3 = 0.765 m^3$	$1 m^3 = 1.31 yd^3$

WOOD	LENGTH	WORKING CONVERSION (HARD)	ACTUAL CONVERSION (SOFT)
	1/32″	1.0 mm	0.8 mm
	1/16″	1.5 mm	1.6 mm
	1/8″	3.0 mm	3.2 mm
	3/16″	5.0 mm	4.8 mm
	1/4″	6.5 mm	6.4 mm
	5/16″	8.0 mm	7.9 mm
	3/8″	9.5 mm	9.5 mm
	7/16″	11.0 mm	11.1 mm
	1/2″	12.5 mm	12.7 mm
	9/16″	14.5 mm	14.3 mm
	5/8″	16.0 mm	15.9 mm
	11/16″	17.5 mm	17.5 mm
	3/4″	19.0 mm	19.1 mm
	13/16″	20.5 mm	20.6 mm
	7/8″	22.0 mm	22.2 mm
	15/16″	24.0 mm	23.8 mm
	1″	25.5 mm	25.4 mm
	2″	50.0 mm	50.8 mm
	4″	100.0 mm	101.6 mm
	6″	150.0 mm	152.4 mm
	8″	200.0 mm	203.02 mm
	10″	250.0 mm	254.0 mm
	12″	300.0 mm	304.8 mm
	1′	300.0 mm	304.8 mm
	2′	600.0 mm	609.6 mm
	4′	1200.0 mm	1219.2 mm
	6′	1800.0 mm	1828.8 mm
	8′	2400.0 mm	2438.4 mm
	10′	3000.0 mm	3048.0 mm
	12′	3600.0 mm	3657.6 mm

DOORS

3'0" X 6'8"	914 mm X 2032 mm
2'8" X 6'8"	812 mm X 2032 mm
2'6" X 6'8"	762 mm X 2032 mm
2'4" X 6'8"	711mm X 2032 mm
2'0" X 6'8"	609 mm X 2032 mm

CONCRETE

PSI	MPA
2175	15.0
2500	17.5
2900	20.0
3625	25.0
3987	27.5

INSULATION FACTOR

R	RSI
R-8	1.4
R-12	2.1
R-20	3.5
R-28	4.8
R-32	5.3
R-40	7.0

GLOSSARY

ACCELERATION CLAUSE

A clause in a mortgage giving the lender the right to declare that the remaining balance of the loan is due immediately; it is usually exercised when the borrower defaults under the mortgage.

ACRE

A unit of land measurement equal to 43 560 square feet, 160 square rods, 10 square chains, or 0.4 hectares.

ADVERSE POSSESSION

An individual, not the owner, takes actual possession of property without the owner's consent.

AGENT

One who is authorized by a principal to represent the principal in business transactions with a third party.

AGREEMENT OF PURCHASE AND SALE

A contract by which one party agrees to sell and another party agrees to purchase.

ANCHOR BOLT

A steel bolt used to secure a structural member against uplift. It is usually deformed at one end to ensure a good grip in the concrete or masonry in which it is embedded.

ANGLE IRON

An L-shaped steel section frequently used to support masonry over a window or door opening.

APPRAISAL

The act or process of estimating value.

ASBESTOS CEMENT

A fire-resisting, weatherproof building material, made from portland cement and asbestos. It is manufactured in several forms such as plain sheets, corrugated sheets, shingles, and pipes.

ATTIC OR ROOF SPACE

The space between the top floor ceiling and roof and between a dwarf partition and sloping roof.

AUTHORITY

The legal power or right conferred under constitutional powers or legal power conferred by delegation from the lawful authority having the right to command or to act.

BACKFILL

The material used to refill an excavation around the outside foundation wall or utility trench.

BALLOON FRAMING

A method of wood-frame construction in which the studs extend in one piece from the foundation sill to the top plate supporting the roof.

BASEBOARD

A moulded board placed against the wall around a room next to the floor to conceal the joint between the floor and wall finish.

BATT

A strip of fibreglass or rock wool insulation pre-cut from four to eight feet long by 15 to 23 inches wide.

BAY WINDOW

A window projecting outside the wall of the house.

BEAM

A horizontal supporting structural member usually wood, steel, or concrete to support vertical loads.

BEAM POCKET

A notch formed at the top of the foundation wall to receive and support the end of a beam.

BEARING

The part of a joist, rafter, truss, or beam which rests on its support and the area of the support on which it rests.

BEARING WALL

A wall that supports any vertical load including its own weight (usually a part of the floors and roof above it).

BOTTOM PLATE

The lower horizontal member of a wood frame wall nailed to the bottom of the wall studs and to the floor framing members.

BRICK VENEER

A facing of brick tied to a wood-frame or masonry wall, serving as a wall covering and carrying no structural loads.

BRIDGING (cross)

Small wood or metal members that are inserted in a diagonal position between adjacent floor or roof joists.

BTU (British Thermal Units)

The quantity of heat required to raise the temperature of one pound of water one degree Fahrenheit.

BUILDING AREA LINE

A line fixed at a certain distance from the front, side, and rear yards, beyond which no building can project.

BUILDING CODE

A collection of regulations established by provincial governments stating standards of construction.

BUILDING PERMIT

A document issued by the municipal authority approving building documents (plans and specifications) for construction and allowing work to commence with conditions.

BUILDING SCHEME

A series of limitations land developers place on the use of building lots within a subdivision.

BUILT-UP ROOF

A roof covering composed of three or more layers of roofing felt or glass fibre saturated with coal tar or asphalt. The top is finished with crushed stone, gravel, or a cap sheet. Generally used on flat or low slope roofs.

BUTT-HINGE

A door hinge used in residential construction.

CANTILEVER

A structural beam, joist, rafter, or truss used for projecting beyond the vertical load bearing line, especially used for extending walls horizontally offset to the vertical load bearing line.

CERAMIC TILES

Vitreous clay tile used for a surface finish.

CERTIFICATE OF OCCUPANCY

A certificate issued by the building department indicating the house is constructed in accordance with the building documents and permission to occupy is granted.

CO ALARM

Carbon monoxide detector which sounds when dangerous levels of carbon monoxide gas are present.

CORNER BEAD

A lightweight metal angle used to shape and reinforce outside corners in drywall and sheetrock construction.

COST-PLUS CONTRACT

A contract in which the owner pays for the actual cost of materials, labor, equipment, and a percentage or fixed fee to cover the builder's overhead and profit. This type of contract is used where the job cannot be accurately estimated because the owner can't or doesn't describe the full extent of the work required in advance. The cost-plus contract is often problematic for the owner because there is little incentive for the builder to carry the work out economically, and the full cost of the house or addition will not be known until the job is complete.

COVENANT

An agreement reduced to writing wherein it is promised certain acts will or will not be performed, or stipulating certain uses or restrictions as to the use of the property.

CRAWL SPACE

A shallow space between the lowest floor of the house and the ground beneath.

CRIBBING

The lining of timber in a shaft.

DAMPPROOFING

The process of coating the outside of a foundation wall with a special preparation to resist passage of moisture through the wall.

DEED

A written document used to convey or transfer real property.

DEED RESTRICTION

An imposed restriction or covenant in a deed or document limiting the present and future owners from using land in a particular way. Also refers to a restrictive covenant or an easement.

DESIGN-BUILD CONTRACT

Where a builder is chosen before the design or plans are prepared. The owner supplies three or four builders with a set of design requirements and the builders, in turn, submit a tender based on preliminary design. This type of contract is suitable where the owner hires an architect or building architectural designer to select from the various proposals.

DEVELOPER

A person or company engaged in the business of subdividing and improving land for resale.

DORMERS

Windows that project from a sloped roof.

DOUBLE GLAZING

Two panes of glass in a door or window, with an air space between the panes. The glass may be sealed hermetically as a single unit or each pane may be installed separately in the door or window sash.

EASEMENT

A right or privilege that one party has in the property of another that entitles the holder to a limited use of the property.

EAVE

The lower part of a roof which projects beyond the face of the walls.

EAVES SOFFIT

The under surface of the eave.

EAVESTROUGH

A trough fixed to an eave which projects beyond the face of the walls.

EFFECTIVE RATE OF INTEREST

The cost of borrowing which includes the rate of interest, brokerage fees, discount, bonus, and other related charges for borrowing.

ENCROACHMENT

An unauthorized intrusion of a building or other improvement, such as a fence, upon the property of the adjoining owner, a sidewalk or a street.

ENCUMBRANCE

An outstanding claim or lien recorded against property owned by another.

EQUITY

The appraised market value of property less all debts against it.

EXTERIOR SIDING

The covering of the exterior walls of a house. It may be made of aluminum, shingles, vinyl, wood, brick, or stone veneer, or other material.

FASCIA BOARD

The flat board enclosing the eaves and roof projections.

FIRE BRICKS

Heat resistant bricks used for lining fireplaces.

FIRE STOP

A complete obstruction placed across a concealed air space in a wall, floor, or roof to retard or prevent the spread of flame or hot gases.

FIRST MORTGAGE

A mortgage that has no recorded predecessor claim or lien.

FIXED PRICE CONTRACT

A fixed price or predetermined lump sum contract sets out the price the owner pays for the scheduled work. This figure could be spread over payments or paid as a lump sum at a predetermined time(s). It means the owner is buying the house or addition at a predetermined price. The fee includes labor, materials, equipment, as well as an allowance for contingencies, overhead, and profit.

FLASHING

Sheet metal or other material used in roof and wall construction to shed water.

FOOTING

A widened section usually concrete, at the base or bottom of a foundation wall, pier, or column.

FOUNDATION

The lower portion, usually concrete or masonry and including the footings, which transfers the weight of, and loads on, a building to the ground.

FRAMING

Sometimes called rough framing, is a type of construction in which the studs, rafters, trusses, joists, sole plates, and roof plates are attached together to form the skeleton of the house.

FROST LINE

The depth below the surface of the earth at which subsurface water may freeze during cold weather. This depth varies from region to region and is set forth by local building codes. Footings must be poured below the frost line.

FURNACE

An enclosed structure in which heat is produced by burning wood, oil, gas, or by electricity. Examples of furnaces are oil, gas, or electric forced air heating units.

GABLE

The upper triangular-shaped portion of the end wall of a house.

GABLE ENDS

The end of a ridged roof.

GIRDER

A large or main beam that supports numerous joists and heavy loads along its span.

GRADE LINE

A pre-determined line indicating the proposed elevation of the ground surface around a building and the property perimeters.

HEADER (framing)

A wood member at right angles to a series of joists or rafters at which the joists or rafters terminate. When used at openings in the floor or roof system the header supports the joist or rafters and acts as a beam.

HEARTH

The floor of the fireplace and immediately in front of it.

HEAT GAIN

Heat transferred into the house from the outside through windows, walls, exterior doors, and ceilings.

HEAT LOSS

Heat escaping from the heated house to the outside through windows, walls, exterior doors, basement, and ceilings.

HIP

The sloping ridge of a roof formed by two intersecting roof slopes.

IMPROVEMENTS

Additions made to the property. This includes the house, in-ground swimming pool, shed, pavements, sidewalks, sewer, water lines, and fences.

INSULATION

Material used to resist heat transmission through walls, floors, and roofs. It may be made of fibreglass, rock-wool, cellulose, or vermiculite.

INTEREST RATE

The amount that lenders charge borrowers for using their money. The most widely used method of charging interest is the annual interest rate, which is a yearly charge stated in the form of a percentage of the loan.

INTERIOR FINISH

The covering used on interior walls and ceilings.

JAMB

The side post or lining of a doorway, window, or other opening.

JOIST

One of a series of horizontal wood members, used to support a floor, ceiling, or roof.

LEASE

Contract between a landlord (lessor) and a tenant (lessee) for the occupation of the landlord's property for a definite period or at will.

LIEN

A legal right or claim that one party (lienor, mortgagee) attaches to the property of another (lienee, mortgagor) that creates an interest in real property as security for payment of a debt or obligation.

LINE OF CREDIT

The maximum amount a bank will lend through a revolving credit account whereby the borrower is free to borrow and repay any amount provided that the outstanding debt does not at any time exceed the line of credit. Larger lines of credit are usually secured by a mortgage.

LINTEL

A horizontal structural member (beam) that supports the load over an opening such as a door or window.

LISTING

An oral or written agreement between a property owner and a broker authorizing the broker to offer the owner's property for sale or lease.

LIVE LOAD

Any load that is not the actual weight of the structure itself. It includes people, furniture, books, wind, and snow.

LOAN-TO-VALUE RATIO

The ratio between the amount of the principal of the mortgage loan and the appraised market value of the property or the purchase price, whichever is lower.

LOOKOUT RAFTERS

Short wood members cantilevered over a wall to support an overhanging portion of a roof.

LUMP SUM

Sometimes called fixed price; a method of payment for construction work whereby the contractor or subcontractor agrees to do specific work for a specific amount of money.

MANSARD ROOF

A roof style of Italian origin, popularized in France.

MANTEL

The decorative framing around a fireplace.

MARKET VALUE

The highest price a property is likely to command if allowed to stay on the market for a reasonable period of time.

MASONRY

Materials constructed of bricks, stones, or concrete.

MECHANIC'S (construction) lien

Rights conferred by virtue of provincial legislation for the benefit of laborers, material suppliers, subcontractors, and contractors, enabling them to register a lien against property to secure payment for work performed or materials furnished to property where the value or condition of the property is improved and the persons entitled to the lien haven't been paid.

METRE

The basic SI (International System) unit of linear measurement. One metre = 39.37 inches.

MINERAL WOOL

A mineral used for insulating buildings, produced by sending a blast of steam through molten slag or rock; common types now in use include rock wool, glass wool, and slag wool.

MITER JOINT

A joint formed by cutting and butting two pieces of board on a line bisecting the angle of their junction.

MORTAR

A substance produced from prescribed proportions of cementing agents, aggregates, and water which gradually sets hard after mixing.

MORTGAGE

A conveyance of property to a creditor (mortgagee) as security for payment of a debt with the right of the debtor (mortgagor) to redeem on payment in full according to the contract terms.

MULTIPLE UNIT DWELLING

A house that includes several separate living units, each accommodating one family, (i.e., a two-family or a four-family dwelling).

NEGATIVE AMORTIZATION

The principal balance of the mortgage loan increases because the monthly payment is insufficient to cover the amount of interest accruing.

OFFER

A promise of a party to do a specific act or give something to another party in return for a specific act or a promise.

ON CENTRE

The distance between the centres of two members that are adjacent to one another. Also centre-to-centre.

OPTION

The right given by the owner of property to another (for valuable consideration) to buy certain property within a limited time at an agreed price.

PARGING

A coat of plaster or cement mortar applied to masonry or concrete walls.

PARTY WALL

A wall constructed on or at the party line between two adjoining lots to serve as the exterior wall for the adjoining houses.

PATIO

A recreational area constructed on the ground.

PITCH

Inclination to the horizontal plane, also known as slope.

PITCHED ROOF

A roof having one or more surfaces sloping at angles greater than necessary for drainage.

PLUMB

Vertical or to make vertical.

PLUMBING

The pipes, fixtures, and other apparatus for the water supply and the removal of waste water.

PORTLAND CEMENT

A hydraulic cement consisting of silica, lime, and alumina intimately mixed in the proper proportions and then burned in a kiln. The clinkers or vetrified product, when finely ground, form an extremely strong cement.

POST

A vertical supporting member.

PREPAYMENT PENALTY

A charge set by lenders for prepaying part or all of the debt before its maturity date.

PRESSURE-TREATED WOOD

Impregnation of wood or plywood with chemicals under pressure to prevent decay and insect (termite) attack.

PRINCIPAL

The amount of the mortgage debt; a main party in a transaction; the homeowner who hires a broker to represent him or her in the sale of their property.

RAFTER

One of the series of structural members of a roof designed to support roof loads.

RAKE

An incline as in a pitched roof. A slope.

RESTRICTED AREA BY-LAW

See Zoning by-law.

RESTRICTIVE COVENANT

A limitation placed on the use of property such as a building scheme devised by land developers.

RUNNING WITH THE LAND

Rights that are binding not only on present owners but on successive owners of the property as with easements and restrictive covenants.

R-VALUE

A measure of the resistance of a building material to heat flow. Higher values indicate greater resistance or better thermal insulating characteristics.

SASH

The frame in which the pane or panes of glass are set in a window; the movable part of the window.

SEALER

A liquid applied directly over uncoated wood for the purpose of sealing the surface.

SECOND MORTGAGE

A mortgage registered against a property which ranks immediately behind a first mortgage determined by the chronological timing of registration.

SEPTIC TANK

A settling tank in which the sludge in the household sewage settles and the affluent discharges into an absorption field or seepage pit.

SETBACK

The minimum distance between the closest point of the outside wall structure to the front, sides, or rear of the property line. Setbacks are established by zoning regulations, deed restrictions, developer's building schemes, and easements.

SHAKES

Shingles made of hand split wood used for roofing and exterior siding.

SHEATHING PAPER

Paper treated with tar or asphalt used under exterior wall cladding as protection against the passage of water or air.

SHED ROOF

A sloping roof having its surface in one plane.

SHINGLES

Small, thin pieces of building materials such as asphalt, wood, or slate used to cover the roof or exterior.

SI (Système international)

The international system of unit measurement intended for use throughout the world. The basic unit of measurement is the metre for linear measurement.

SIDE YARD

The minimum distance between the side wall of the house and the property lines facing them, as set forth in zoning regulations, building schemes, and easements.

SIDING

In wood-frame construction, the material other than masonry or stucco used as an exterior wall covering.

SILL

The horizontal member forming the bottom of an opening such as a door or window.

SILL PLATE

A structural member anchored to the top of the foundation wall, upon which the floor joists rest.

SINGLE-FAMILY HOUSE

A house that is designed for the occupancy of one family only.

SMOKE ALARM

An electrical device which sounds an alarm when sensing the presence of products of combustion.

SOFFIT

The underside covering of the eave overhang.

SPAN

The distance between the structural supports of beams and girders.

SPECIFIC PERFORMANCE

An equitable remedy granted by courts to compel a party to specifically perform the terms of a contract. An example is where a purchaser asks the court to force a vendor to specifically transfer property to him or her according to the terms of the contract.

STATUTE OF LIMITATIONS

A law setting the maximum period of time during which a lawsuit may be filed after the occurrence of the cause of the suit.

STEP FLASHING

Rectangular or square pieces of flashing used at the junction of shingled roof or walls. Also called shingle flashing.

STRIKE PLATE

The part of a door lock set fastened to the jamb.

STRINGERS

The sloping sides of a stair flight that support the treads and risers; small beams.

STUCCO

A covering for exterior and interior walls applied in the form of a plastic mortar or paste that hardens in a few days. The paste mix for exterior walls consists of portland cement, sand, and lime.

STUDS

Vertical members in wall framing. Their function is to form the wall and support the floors and the roof above them.

SUBFLOOR

Plywood, particle board, or boards nailed together to the floor joists to form a base for the finish floor.

SUBORDINATION CLAUSE

A clause of an agreement where a second mortgage lender allows the mortgagor to refinance a new mortgage loan which will rank in priority, notwithstanding that the position of the second mortgage is first in order of time registration.

SUMP

A small reservoir to collect water usually in the basement that is discharged by a pump.

SURVEY

A report and drawing prepared to scale showing the lengths and directions of the boundary lines, surrounding property, and streets; the positioning of the house, easements, encroachments, exterior improvements such a fences, sheds, driveway etc.

TAPING

The process of covering drywall joints with paper tape and glossing over with approximately three coats of joint compound to produce a continuous smooth surface.

TERM

The time by the end of which the mortgage loan must be paid in full or a new term negotiated.

THREE-WAY SWITCH

A switch used in house wiring when a light (lights) is controlled from two places. A three-way switch must be used at each location.

THRESHOLD

A strip of wood, metal, or other material bevelled on each edge and used at the junction of two different floor finishes under doors, or on top of the door sill at exterior doors.

TIME IS OF THE ESSENCE

A clause in a contract requiring punctual performance related to the terms of the contract.

TITLE SEARCH

An examination of the public records to discover the owners name registered on the title abstract or register and the names of other parties who have an interest in the real property disclosed by instruments registered affecting the quality of title.

TOPOGRAPHY

That which indicates the configuration of the earth's surface and the locations of the natural or man-made monuments.

TOP PLATE

The horizontal member nailed to the top of the partition or wall studs.

TREAD

The horizontal part of a step.

TRIM

Finish carpentry, including the installation of interior door jambs, baseboard, window and door casings, closet shelving, hardware, fireplace mantel, railing, mouldings, and hardware.

VALLEY

The internal angle formed where two sloping roofs intersect from different directions.

VALLEY RAFTERS

Rafters that are located at the centre of roof valleys to support the jack rafters.

VALUATION

Estimated worth or price. The act of ascertaining how much specific real property is worth.

VAPOR BARRIER

Material used for retarding the passage of moisture and air.

VENDOR

A seller of real property.

WALL PLATES

In wood-frame construction, the horizontal members attached to the ends of the studs. Also called top or bottom plates, depending on their location.

WATER TABLE

The level below which the ground is saturated with water.

WEATHERSTRIPPING

Strips of felt, rubber, metal, or other material, fixed along the edges of doors or windows to keep out drafts and reduce heat loss.

WEEPHOLE

Small holes located at the bottom of retaining walls or masonry veneer walls to drain water to the exposed face.

ZONING BY-LAW

A by-law passed by a municipality prohibiting the use of land in certain areas for any purpose other than as set out in the by-law. Sometimes referred to as a restricted area by-law.